Sit, Ubu, Sit

How I Went from Brooklyn to Hollywood
with the Same Woman,
the Same Dog, and a Lot Less Hair

Sit, Ubu, Sit

GARY DAVID GOLDBERG

Harmony Books
New York

Published in the United States by Harmony Books, an imprint of the Crown Publishing
Group, a division of Random House, Inc., New York.
www.crownpublishing.com

Except for the obvious and the famous, most of the names within have been changed,
primarily to make it easier for people who may not have wished to appear in my life story.

Harmony Books is a registered trademark and the Harmony Books colophon is a
trademark of Random House, Inc.

Library of Congress Cataloging-in-Publication Data

Goldberg, Gary David.
  Sit, Ubu, sit / Gary David Goldberg.—1st ed.
    1. Goldberg, Gary David.   2. Television producers and directors—United
States—Biography.   3. Television writers—United States—Biography.   I. Title.
  PN1992.4.G65A3 2008
  791.4502'3092—dc22
  [B]   2007023061

ISBN 978-0-307-39418-7

Printed in the United States of America

All photos from the collection of Gary David Goldberg

DESIGN BY ELINA D. NUDELMAN

10 9 8 7 6 5 4 3 2 1

First Edition

For Diana, of course.
As with all things.

Who knew it would
turn out this way

You can put the Frisbee down now, Ubu.
Good dog.

1985

I've never been to a psychic before and, I have to admit, I feel a little nervous. I don't know what I'm expecting exactly, but this isn't it. For one thing, I'm waiting in her kitchen, right now, while she's downstairs finishing her laundry. I didn't know psychics did their own laundry.

When she's done, she comes into the kitchen, sits down across from me, and smiles. Her age is anywhere from twenty-three to seventy-five, and I immediately feel as if I may actually be in the presence of someone with a strong spiritual connection to the universe. I live in California now, and I've been assured it's OK to have these feelings. I grew up in Brooklyn, and the closest I ever came to a psychic was my uncle Morris, who claimed that he could see the future and "it stinks."

She puts out a deck of cards, asks me to cut, turns over one pile, and begins laying out the cards. She looks up at me a moment, then she laughs. "Why do you feel so guilty about having all this money?" I feel a jolt of electricity go through my body. This is, in fact, the reason I have come to see her.

With the syndication of our television series, *Family Ties,* Diana and I have, suddenly, become extremely wealthy, and for the first time in our sixteen years together, our relationship is threatened. We're a little distant. Awkward. Not the usual loving and thoughtful manner we have toward each other. In the upscale neighborhood where we now live, behind huge iron gates, I'm in a lawsuit with every one of my neighbors. Determined, I guess, to prove I don't belong there.

Diana and I have no romantic construct for being wealthy people. There's nothing "sexy" about it, for us. It was never a value. Never a goal. And it happened kind of accidentally. We're not quite sure who we are in this new role. Whether we like ourselves as much.

"I don't know why I feel guilty. I just do."

"Before you came into this world, you made a commitment to feed and nurture and care for families and children. It's right that you have all this money. The universe wants you to be happy."

She is so much better than Uncle Morris.

"You'll do the right thing with it, don't worry. And, it's OK to enjoy yourself. You're supposed to."

For a first reading, this is going very well, I think, and at the end of the session, I thank her and I rise to go. We shake, and she holds my hand, tightly, in hers.

"There's one more message from the universe for you. Very important."

"What's that?"

"Never leave the woman you're with. You're nothing without her."

I nod and smile.

"I know."

1972

{chapter one}

We're walking down the street in Athens and it's hot. Like in the *Iliad* hot. There are three of us. Me, Diana, and Ubu, our Labrador retriever. We've been hitchhiking around the world for ten months now, and we're trying to make our way back up to Brussels to catch a student flight over to America. Ubu, who prides himself on never having been on a leash, walks a few paces ahead. He has his big city face on. "Don't try to pet me. Don't tell me how cute I am. We're on official business."

Actually, we're on our way to the Red Cross to give blood. We're almost completely out of money and we'll be getting ten dollars, a glass of orange juice, and a shower. Diana, who is four months pregnant and will not be giving blood, will get the orange juice and the shower. She's excited. She can't believe she's going to get fresh juice. I can't believe we're going to get ten bucks.

The Red Cross building looks more like a souvlaki stand, but judging by the crowd gathered out in front, today's "shower-juice-American-money combo" is turning out to be a real winner. We recognize a lot of the faces from around town. The American Express office, Syntagma Square. Everyone in their early to mid twenties. Brightly dressed and covered in bangles and beads. Could be a casting call for *Hair.*

They welcome us into the line and we all smile, hug, do the peace sign, nod and mumble some "hey mans," and offer each other fruits and nuts. I've come to really love and admire this floating community of gentle people we've become a part of. Wherever we've gathered, from Amsterdam to Istanbul, everyone's been open and extremely generous. Willing to share everything they have, down to the very last grain of brown rice.

As we get closer to the Red Cross building, I may be imagining it, but I can swear I hear moaning coming from inside. Diana gives my hand a squeeze. "You're tough. You can do this." I'm surprised she thinks I can be so easily manipulated. And disappointed in myself when I realize that it's working.

We edge our way forward, but at the front door we're stopped and told that Ubu has to wait outside. Though not happy, Ubu takes this in stride. On some level he was expecting it. With a big yawn of disapproval, he lies down obediently. But then at the very last moment, he sticks one paw defiantly back into the room. He's becoming passive aggressive. I make a note to talk to him about this.

The nurse, a fortyish woman, is like every other Greek person we've ever met, unfailingly friendly and sweet. Her English is equivalent to my Greek and we quickly realize we have no idea what we're saying to each other. It doesn't matter. We're young. We're in Greece. And I'm about to give blood in a souvlaki stand. Diana gives my hand another squeeze. She really wants that juice.

We move farther into the room and I'm seated now on a little cot. I'm next in line and the guy in front of me, who's being poked at the moment, is not very happy. I hear him shout "merde" several times and, even though I flunked French twice in college, I know what that means.

The guy's becoming more agitated by the moment, and, amazingly, his coloring is beginning to resemble that of the Greek flag—blue on a white background. He begins screaming in a language that I'm pretty sure is French, bearing in mind that I did flunk it twice, and he's speaking rapidly, and I think he wants to know, "Where is the train station?"

For the first time, the idea of me fainting rears its ugly head. The fact that it's 115 degrees in this room and smells like we're inside a diesel engine is not helping. Diana gives me a little kiss for comfort. "You'll be fine."

When I regain consciousness, I'm on a blanket out in the alley. Ubu is there with me, as is Diana. Ubu gives me his "you're still my guy" look and a little lick. Diana gives me the same look without the lick. I notice that her hair is wet and she has the remnants of a cute little orange juice mustache. She holds up a ten dollar bill and she smiles. My work here is done.

In the evening we return to our campsite, which is in a park on a hill across from the Acropolis. In the morning, if you get up early enough before it opens, you can race up the four thousand steps to the top of the Parthenon, and you get to use the bathrooms there for free. While there are NO CAMPING ALLOWED signs scattered prominently throughout this park, in typical Greek fashion these signs are not enforced. We did get one "official" visit from two policemen yesterday. But that was only to alert us they had to do their weekly "sweep" and we should be out of the park between eight and ten but we could return at ten fifteen and put the tent back up and they're sorry to bother us and they love California.

It was Diana who introduced me to the world of camping and the great outdoors. Growing up in Brooklyn, we were not really tuned in to the glories of nature and rarely experienced it firsthand. The closest you'd get was when someone told you to "take a fuckin' hike."* But I have to say, I love it now. And in the ten months we've been on the road, I think we've slept indoors eight times.

On the island of Mykonos, we split the outdoor/indoor difference, living in a cave carved into the hillside above Paradise Beach. We had two "rooms" there. Or, actually, "one plus an alcove," is

---

*This insight actually belongs to Larry David, and I've taken it from a speech he gave to the NRDC (Natural Resources Defense Council) in 2004. It's reproduced here with his kind permission. Larry, like all comedy writers, is from Brooklyn.

how the ad would read. We put down a rug. Hung up a madras bedspread. Forty-five hundred dollars a month in New York.

We wait for sunset now to have our dinner. This evening I'm getting a little extra attention from Ubu and Diana. They know that tonight's meal was bought with my blood, so to speak. And they want me to know how much they appreciate it.

Diana and I are vegetarians, not from any great moral concerns but rather the fact that meat's just too expensive. Ubu has not completely bought into this program, and while Diana slices vegetables, he gnaws on some stick meat he's been schlepping with him since Corfu. Without realizing, I must be looking longingly at the meat, because Ubu picks it up and moves over to the other side of Diana where he feels more safe.

Before we took off on this trip, everyone we knew had warned us, "You can't bring a dog to Europe." And, you certainly can't hitchhike with a dog. Crushed by the Nixon presidency and his policies, we had only purchased one-way tickets, not sure when, or if, we would be coming back. There was no way we were leaving Ubu behind.

It turned out to be a relatively simple matter to get him over here. Just a series of shots, which Ubu received stoically, Labrador style. A letter from our vet. And though he had to travel cargo, something for which he's not yet truly forgiven us, and we had to stand around at the airport while he did a twenty-three-minute piss when he was let out of his crate, he otherwise arrived without incident.

As far as hitchhiking goes, most people who pick us up, pick us up because of Ubu. Sometimes, they put us in the back and ask Ubu to sit up front with them. Those are his favorite rides. And I have to admit, he does know his role in those situations. He will give a paw when asked. Give a kiss. And on a long ride in a comfortable car he will put head in lap and allow himself to be adored and loved, complimented on the softness of his fur and the beauty of his eyes. Behavior I would come to recognize later in certain television stars I'd get to work with.

The lights are coming on now at the Acropolis. Diana has spread out a beautiful batik tablecloth she made while we were living on a kibbutz in Israel. She has an artist's eye for shape and color, and she's brought an instinctive elegance and style to our vagabond life. No matter what we're having, she will always put out napkins, silverware, and light a candle. It seems like overkill tonight when dinner is an eggplant, but that boarding-school training dies hard.

Diana and I have been together three years now. The first time I saw her was at my friend Ben's apartment in Brooklyn. She was seated cross-legged on the floor playing the guitar. Long hair, beautiful green eyes, she was a stewardess for Pan American, and she wasn't Jewish. "Yes, one of those," I thought. "I'd like that."

After she finished her song, I had to maneuver my way through a large group of guys who obviously felt the same way I did, but eventually I found myself standing next to her.

"Nice guitar," I said.

A lame beginning to a relationship that was going to last a lifetime, but you have to start somewhere.

"Martin," she said, looking up at me.

"My name's Gary."

"The guitar. It's a Martin."

I revise my plan to pass myself off as a musician between gigs who works in a bookstore at night and wants to be a kindergarten teacher, which I sense would work with her. In point of fact, I am a waiter at the Village Gate, a jazz club on Bleecker Street. I'm twenty-five, a part-time actor, I've been kicked out of two colleges, as well as deselected from the Peace Corps, and I've never earned enough money in any one year to file an income tax return. But I'm not sure I should lead with that.

"I know who you are," she says.

"Really?"

"Yes. I've been warned about you by several of your friends."

I make a note to get new friends.

"Why? What'd they say?"

"They said you were cute. But, they also said you're self-centered, shallow, and vain."

"Perhaps we need to hear from my enemies."

She smiled and she was so beautiful my knees went weak.

We agree to meet the next afternoon, not a date, nothing as serious as that. Just me, a New York native, wanting to show her, recently transferred here, some of my favorite sights in the Big Apple. The problem is, I have no favorite sights. Although I've lived in New York all my life, I've never been to the Empire State Building or the Statue of Liberty, and with Ebbets Field no longer there and Coney Island no longer safe, my favorite sights come down to Madison Square Garden and Eddie Sukenick's apartment, which has color TV.

At the Gate that night I ask Leon, one of the older guys, for help. I explain that I think I've met someone "above my station" and I want to know a "classy" place that I can take her. A place that will say I'm surprisingly sensitive, though obviously heterosexual. That there's more to me than meets the eye, which I think will be my slogan.

"What about the Cloisters?"

"I can't afford a restaurant."

"It's a museum up in Fort Tryon Park. An old convent, beautiful grounds, unicorn tapestries, antiques. Tranquil yet sensual."

I'm hoping I won't fall asleep there but it sounds promising. Maybe that's who I am. Tranquil yet sensual. Maybe that's my slogan.

The Cloisters is absolutely gorgeous. Set high up in the middle of the park. The main building is made up of portions of four medieval cloisters, which have been integrated into a museum. Hard to believe Yankee Stadium is only half a mile away.

Inside the beautiful Romanesque chapel, the paintings and the tapestries are spectacular. We rest for a moment in front of its most famous acquisition, the seven unicorn tapestries. It's unbelievably quiet. And oddly enough, it is tranquil yet sensual. Diana speaks in appropriately hushed tones.

"It's so beautiful here."

"I know."

"Do you come here a lot?"

"I do."

I can see her revising her opinion of me even as we speak. I look dramatically off into the middle distance.

"There's a tranquillity here I find satisfying. A special peace. I sometimes think I'm more myself here than anywhere else I know."

I may have gone too far but no, when I look back she's still seated. She gives my arm a squeeze. I have the decency to say no more.

We're standing outside now in the beautiful gardens, looking out across the Hudson to the New Jersey cliffs. The sun is setting in what I now realize must be the west but I've always thought of as the north.

"Thank you for bringing me here."

She puts her arm through mine and snuggles closer. I make a note to send Leon flowers.

We stand there silently for one lovely perfect moment, then she pulls apart.

"You've never been here before, have you?

"No. Not really."

"I didn't think so."

She nods and smiles sweetly. Somehow that was the right answer and somehow reassuring. We resume snuggling and watch the sun go down either in the north or in the west.

Twenty-five years later we will return to this exact spot with our second daughter, who was then eleven.

"This is it. This is the spot where Mom and Dad had our first date. Where we had our first kiss."

She looks like she's going to be ill, tries to force a smile.

"I *so* don't want to be here."

1954

{ c h a p t e r t w o }

"*D*on't let him get behind you."

My brother's words come out in puffy little clouds this cold December day in Brooklyn.

"Look at me."

He knows I'm not listening. I'm dreaming of glory. I'm ten years old, I'm in fourth grade, and I'm playing football on my brother's team. He's fifteen, a freshman in high school. He's my hero. I'm going to intercept this pass and run it back for a touchdown. Make him proud.

"We can give up the short pass. That's OK. Just keep everything in front of you."

I'm nodding my head as if I'm listening, but I'm already doing the postgame interview with Marty Glickman.

"I owe it all to my brother, Stanley. He's the one who gave me the chance, Marty. He's the one who always believed in me."

That part's true. My brother always looks out for me. Tries to include me. Some of his friends don't like it.

"Why's your kid brother always have to play?"

My brother defends me. He's the leader of this group so whatever he says goes. And he says I get to play. A couple of these guys don't like me because even though I'm only ten and they're fifteen, I'm a better ballplayer than they are. And they know it. One of the reasons they know it is because I've told them.

The other team breaks their huddle now, and we fall into our defensive positions. I have been hiking the ball for three hours straight, the price you pay to play with the "big guys," which consists of me hiking the ball, then getting punched in the head and pushed on my ass by whoever's playing over me, and this is my reward for getting pummeled for the better part of a Saturday morning. I get to play one play at defensive back.

"Don't let him get behind you."

"Right."

Flanked out to my side now comes Bobby Beradino, my archenemy, my Lex Luthor. He's the guy who complains the most about me hangin' around. One day last year, when I was still in third grade, we were sitting on the stoop in front of Butchie Friedberg's house, and Beradino got up and announced he was going home to jerk off. "Yeah, me too," I said, getting to my feet. I had no idea what jerking off was, but I felt, if Bobby Beradino could do it, so could I. And I could do it better.

"Do you even know what you're talking about?" my brother asked.

When I confessed I didn't, he explained to me what it meant and what was actually involved in masturbation.

"You're kidding? Why would anybody do that? Anyway, you're not allowed to touch yourself 'down there.' Mommy told me."

Beradino takes up his position at right end, does a snorty little laugh when he sees I'm the one who's going to be covering him, and he calls over to the quarterback, Anthony Morelli, and they both point to me, as if to say, let's go after the kid. Anthony Morelli's famous in the neighborhood for having beaten up one of the after-school counselors one day, when the guy tried to take away his comb. He's also famous for having an older brother who is actually in jail, where Anthony will soon be joining him, no doubt. And for having the biggest hands anyone has ever seen.

Beradino's wearing pointy black hoodlum shoes with taps on the bottom. The kind my mother will never let me get. I'm wearing my all-white Keds. This is no longer just a game of touch football. This is a battle between good and evil.

The ball is snapped and there's a frenzy of motion. Beradino comes out about five yards and buttonhooks. Morelli looks over and starts to throw the ball his way. I'm right behind him waiting. This is going to be too easy. And as Morelli's arm comes forward, I dash in front of Beradino, ready to make the interception, except Morelli doesn't throw the ball. It's a pump fake. No one in fourth grade can pump-fake. No one can throw a forward pass. Morelli pulls the ball back and Bobby Beradino is now behind me. The one place I promised my brother he would never be.

I take off after him but it's too late. Morelli arches the ball over my head, and it's drifting lazily into the waiting arms of a laughing Bobby Beradino, when out of the corner of my eye, I see my brother come flying across the schoolyard, leave his feet, dive at Beradino, and at the very last second, my brother tips the ball away, and it falls harmlessly to the ground. I come running over. Panting. I'm trying not to cry. My brother's dungarees are ripped. His nose is bleeding. He looks up at me.

"What'd I tell you?"

We live in the Bensonhurst section of Brooklyn, between Bay Ridge and Coney Island. The neighborhood is predominantly Jewish and Italian. It will turn out such distinguished and diverse alumni as Larry King, Sandy Koufax, and Sammy "The Bull" Gravano. Growing up in Bensonhurst and then finding myself later in show business, I'm familiar with two elements of American life purported not to exist—the Mafia and Q scores for actors. I've seen both. It's hard to say which has wreaked more havoc on the fabric of society, though I lean toward Q scores.

The Jews and the Italians coexist, relatively peacefully most of the time, but chasing of Jews is not unheard of. I don't know how these guys find the time to chase Jews so much. Don't they have homework?

My brother tells me what I need to do.

"You can't back down and you can't run. They're going to catch you anyway, and it only makes it more fun for them. If they get you, you have to fight back."

With knees quaking and voice shaking I try to stand my ground when cornered. "Yes, you can beat me up." And yes, in the end, "you will win and inflict pain." But, "it will take you longer to beat me up than somebody else." Not words to rally a nation by, I grant you, but strangely effective here.

The older guys will still stop me, push me around a little, scare the hell out of me, but then they'll let me go. Not worth the effort. Just like Stanley said. And a good lesson about how to deal with bullies. In Bensonhurst or in Hollywood. Diana feels that much of my life has been devoted to trying to prove that Jewish guys are as tough as Italian guys. Which, by the way, we're not. Unless we're in Israel and they're in World War II.

One day, on my way to the grocery store to get a loaf of bread, I'm stopped by Patsy DiPasquale. Patsy's in seventh grade, looks to be about twenty-three or twenty-four, and it's rumored that he's married and has two kids.

"Where you goin', Jewboy?"—said with affection in my memory.

"I'm going to Wolkoff Brothers to get a rye bread, which is a food of my people."

I'm trying to enlarge the purpose of my trip to the grocery store, giving it some biblical perspective, imbuing it with a noble purpose of nourishing not just my own family, but all the people of Judea and Samaria. I've pointed out to Patsy several times that Jesus himself was Jewish. That the early Christians were probably all Jews, except maybe Paul, who claimed he was a Roman, but did, in fact, change his name from Saul, so who knows. And Patsy himself, somewhere deep in his own ancestry, might very well be part Jewish. Patsy doesn't seem to give a shit.

"Lemme have your money."

"I can't. I have to get the rye bread. I told you."

"How much you got on you?"

"I've got a quarter."

I take it out of my pocket to show him.

"Rye bread's only nineteen cents. Gimme that."

He takes the quarter out of my hand. Searches through his pockets and gives me back nineteen cents, keeping six for himself. I'm being held up by a guy who makes change. But Patsy understood the "rules." He had to keep me viable as what we would later come to call a "revenue stream." If I came home without a rye bread, there'd be an investigation. Patsy had to know I'd "crack." Six cents was better than nothing, and we'd both get to play another day. Eventually, the game stopped when I got bigger than Patsy, and faster.

Patsy died in Vietnam.

Bensonhurst, Brooklyn, in 1954 is a paradise for two sports-crazed boys like my brother and myself. Sports is all we care about. All we talk about. There's not a book in our house. Not a magazine. We read the *Daily News,* starting from the back, where the sports section is, and when we're done with that part, we close the paper and put it away.

The *New York Times* may as well be printed in Sanskrit for all the influence it has in our neighborhood. I see it lying there on the counter at the candy store next to the *News* and the *Mirror* and the *Post.* Seems very pleased with itself. Like it knows that it's important. But to buy the *Times* would be to make a statement. That you thought you were too good for the neighborhood. That you were showing off. That you were trying to be "somebody."

We live in the same building with my grandparents, my mother's parents, Jake and Jenny, who live downstairs. My grandpa Jake would easily win the award as the world's sweetest, kindest man if it weren't for my father, who's the world's other sweetest, kindest man. And, of course, my brother, the world's sweetest, kindest, younger man. And so it's a three-way tie there at the top.

Grandpa used to own a hat company named after my brother, "Stanley Hats." But when the workers decided to go out on strike, after some deliberation Grandpa decided they were right, and joined them. This confused everybody for a while and really screwed up their sing-alongs about worker solidarity. And then the company went bankrupt. It's still a case study at Harvard Business School under "Hat Company: How Not to Run One."

Any push for achievement or success (outside the sports world) comes from the female side. My mother is a brilliant woman who graduated at the top of her class in high school but never went to college. Her teachers came to the house to beg Grandpa to let her continue, but money was tight. Mom was a near genius at math and much sought after as a bookkeeper in the millinery trade, where Grandpa worked, and they needed her salary.

She's in charge of all academic matters. If I get a 98 on a test she always asks, "What happened to the other two points?" If I get an A, why not A-plus? She always reads my homework, makes notes, routinely changes what I've written. This will turn out to be good training for my future career writing for TV and film.

But it's my grandma Jenny who is the real power in the family. In the building. In the neighborhood. In the borough. And, through some nephews and cousins she controls, her influence extends into Queens and two apartment buildings in the Bronx. She can't read English; she can barely write her own name. In her whole life she's spent a total of a half a day in school. But she is without a doubt the smartest person I will ever know. "A woman of valor," my father calls her. Admiration, mixed with just a touch of fear, which is how she likes it.

Jenny understands instinctively about power. How to get it. How to use it. How to keep it. And she controls all access to the outside world. She has a telephone. We don't have one. We can use hers. She has a television set. We don't have one. We can use hers. She has a car, which she will never learn to drive. We don't have one. We can use hers. So if you want to talk to anyone, watch anything or go anywhere, you have to go through her. Not bad for half a day in school. She must have really been paying attention.

The lack of a phone in our apartment is becoming a problem for my brother. He's fifteen and beginning to get calls from girls. It starts with Grandma yelling up from downstairs, "Stanley, telephone. A girl." This announcement causes other doors in the building to open, so the neighbors can offer up their sage advice and encouragement to my brother on his journey to speak with a girl, which somehow has become a community event.

"Ask about her parents."

"Don't chew and talk at the same time."

And finally Mr. Koplowitz below: "Don't do it. Leave the girls alone. They'll ruin your life"—until his wife would drag him back inside.

Once inside Grandma's apartment and actually on the telephone, Stanley still had to deal with Grandma herself, who would sit across from him, arms folded, watching, as he began his conversation.

"Can I have some privacy, please?" he would ask.

This was a concept not much valued in our neighborhood.

"Privacy," Grandma would shoot back, as if that one word embodied all the ills of the modern world. "What? You have secrets from the family? Who are you, Julius and Ethel Rosenberg?"

Making this request for privacy, an act of betrayal so heinous that you couldn't be simply Julius *or* Ethel Rosenberg. You had to be both. In case one of them got off, posthumously, on a technicality.

I benefit a lot from being Stanley Goldberg's little brother. Everybody assumes that I'm as nice as he is, though I'm really not. I'm an emotional child. I cry easily. Movies. Books. If the Dodgers lose. Anything to do with animals. My mother says I'm sensitive. Bobby Beradino says I'm a homo.

On Sunday nights we gather downstairs at Grandma's to watch Ed Sullivan. It was the one night my dad, who worked a lot of double shifts at the post office, would always be home.

"Anyone want to . . . ," he would begin.

"Get ice cream," I would yell.

"I was going to say go to sleep early."

And we'd all laugh, even though we'd been playing these same parts for years now. Dad always gave it his all and was, in his own way, a much better performer than Ed Sullivan.

Stanley and I would run out the door with the ice-cream orders, always the same orders, ringing in our ears. Everybody would call out different and exotic flavors, at first. "Pistachio." "Black Walnut." "Mocha Almond Fudge." The boldness of their choices echoed in the halls so everyone could see that they were not afraid. That they were ready to participate fully in all the opportunities this new land of America had to offer. And then, at the last minute, the changing of their minds, prudence prevailing, not quite ready for that much "experimenting," falling back on what was tried and true. On what was known.

"Wait . . . vanilla," from Grandpa.

"Vanilla," from my dad.

"Vanilla," from Mom.

And then from Grandma, "Chocolate . . . , no, vanilla."

No ice cream would ever taste that sweet again. Ever.

Almost forty years later I would do a television show, *Brooklyn Bridge,* about my grandma. About our family. About our neighborhood, where we were everybody's children and they were all our parents. My grandma, who had outlived her husband and all her children, was in her nineties then, still very alert, still very sharp. I asked her how she liked the show. She liked it.

"You made me look very pretty."

I was glad she liked it. And she *was* very pretty, I reminded her. She smiled a little thank-you.

"You know those two boys on the show?"

"Yes, Grandma?"

"You weren't that good."

1972

{ c h a p t e r   t h r e e }

*D*iana, Ubu, and I have hitched our way easily out of Greece and up through Yugoslavia, but we're stuck now in the south of France, a little town called Saint Louis. We're trying to get to Paris to meet up with one of my old teachers, Dr. Goldberger. She's at the Sorbonne and has invited us to spend a few days with her and her family. A gifted teacher, she encouraged me to attend to my more "artistic" side, when I wasn't even sure I had one. But we have a rapidly closing window, because today is Monday and we have to be in Brussels on Thursday to make our student flight back to New York.

We've been in Saint Louis for three days, unable to get a ride out, and it has occurred to me that we may actually die here. Not that any of the townspeople would notice. This is the height of De Gaulle's anti-Americanism, and the locals are not shy about show-ing their displeasure. Cars full of French families speed by with eighty-year-old Frenchwomen giving us the finger. "Show them what we think of Americans, *Grand-mère*!" And up will come another gnarled middle digit.

We play Frisbee on the side of the road. Throw a softball back and forth. Work with Ubu on "sit" and "stay" in French. Diana and I are together twenty-four hours a day on this trip. We provide our own entertainment. Diana sings, does arts and crafts. I do book reports, mainly history and biography. This trip has featured my reports on Oppenheimer, Einstein, and Freud. It's the "Smart Jews Tour" of Europe.

We're our own world and depend on each other for everything. A pattern that would continue throughout our life. Even later, when I achieved some small amount of public success, it never really mattered. It was never really real to me until I could bring it home to Diana and she could validate it. I was always, am always, writing for an audience of one.

As dusk falls, we give up for the day and start back through the town toward our campsite up the hill. The main square is lovely. Every brick and stone in celestial harmony. Every design element perfect. They may be mean bastards, the French, but they do have style.

We stop in front of a cozy bistro at one end of the square and peer in through the window. The tables are set, the candles are lit, the evening's specials marked on the chalkboard by the bar. Altogether lovely and inviting.

"You go here tonight."

A softly accented female voice causes us to turn around. We see a fashionably dressed woman in her mid-fifties, looks like Claudette Colbert. She's smiling. We didn't know French people were allowed to smile.

"No, no."

I laugh, and take out a package of Knorr's dried soup.

"Soup we make. Dinner to have."

I don't know why, but I'm suddenly speaking like I don't know English. The fashionable lady laughs. Diana laughs. Ubu smiles.

"No." The woman repeats. "You go here tonight."

And we realize it's not a question. She points to me and Diana and to the restaurant and motions for us to go inside.

"I will pay. Yes?"

She ushers us into the restaurant, speaks in hushed tones to the proprietor, who smiles (another French smile; it's an epidemic now) and then leads us over to a table by the window. The generous

27

French lady gives us a wave and goes to join friends waiting at another table. Three men and a woman. She must be telling them "the story" because they look over at us and raise a glass. We wave. Ubu barks. This is what he thought France would be like.

The rest of the night's a blur. A montage of wine and cheese and crème brûlée and sauces and chickens and cognacs. An overwhelming feeling of affection for the whole human race. At one point I declare I will apply for French citizenship.

She never even told us her name. One time when we looked up, she was about to leave. She gave us a final, almost shy, little wave. And a night we'd remember for the rest of our lives.

In the morning, we decide to spend our last remaining dollars on train tickets up to Paris. We'll be arriving completely broke, but I'm sure Dr. Goldberger will be more than happy to loan us the few dollars we'll need to get up to Brussels to catch our plane. I don't want to miss a chance to see her and for her to meet Diana and Ubu.

When we get to Paris, I call the number Dr. Goldberger has given us. I dial carefully, our last centimes, and when someone picks up, in my best French I ask, *"Excusez-moi, Madame Goldberger, s'il vous plaît."* I'm not sure if I'm hearing correctly, because this voice seems to be saying that Madame Goldberger is not there. That she is not coming. I immediately drop my French.

"What do you mean she's not coming?"

The voice also switches to English almost accent-free.

"There was an airline strike. It was in all the papers. She comes next week. Hello . . . hello."

At the American Embassy, they're polite but firm. It's not possible to advance money under any circumstances.

"My father works in the post office. You can attach his salary."

"Why don't you try Travelers Aid? They're set up for people like you."

We ignore the obvious slur and head over to Travelers Aid, where we do, in fact, see a lot of "people like us." Many of the same people we saw giving blood in Athens, as a matter of fact, and we all smile, hug, do the peace sign, nod and mumble some "hey mans," and offer each other fruits and nuts.

Travelers Aid is basically like the old TV game show *Queen for a Day*. You come in and tell your story to the panel, and if it's sufficiently pathetic, you get some money. I figure we have a pretty strong hand. Pregnant national merit finalist, son of a civil servant, trusty Labrador retriever. And, all we're really asking for is a place to stay for one night and money for the train up to Brussels tomorrow. We can sleep in the airport there tomorrow night.

The three-judge panel is composed of two fortyish women who are or were or should be nuns. And an older man, polite, quiet. He seems Jewish to me, but all polite and quiet older men seem Jewish to me, so I'm not sure. In any case, I feel Diana and I are covered, given our diverse backgrounds. And, let's face it, at this point we're willing for Diana to be bar-mitzvahed, if it'll get us up to Brussels.

We tell our story, and in the end it all boils down to this. They're worried about Ubu. They don't seem overly concerned about me and Diana, even the possibly Jewish guy, who I was really counting on. But the thought of a dog in any peril has gotten their attention. Ubu somehow senses this and has sauntered over close to the two ladies and let it be known he's available for petting, should they feel the need. He has incredible emotional intelligence and may, in fact, be some sort of genius. I make a note to have him tested when we get home.

In the end, it's a complete win for our team. We get a room for the night, five dollars to spend any way we want, and train tickets up to Brussels. Ubu gets a bag of dog treats just for himself, and some new chew toys.

That night we walk around the magical city. And, while it may be true you can *see* Paris for five dollars a day, you can't actually touch it. But tonight it doesn't matter. We walk hand in hand along the Seine, overcome with happiness. Excitement about our baby yet to come.

We have no money. No earthly possessions. No place to live when we get back. But we are somehow, and for some reason, supremely confident about our future. I think on some level it may be that we suspect we've each found the other half of our souls. That we've found our life partners and that we'll keep each other safe. Maybe it's the five bucks.

In the morning, we take one last walk around Paris. Diana takes a picture of Ubu near the Louvre that will become the logo for the production company we'll start in just about ten years. I love that picture. I love that Diana took it. And it always reminds me how little distance I want between who I was that day and who I am now.

In the afternoon, we make our way up to Brussels to catch our plane back to the States. But there's still one more hurdle we have to clear. We have no money to get Ubu home. Even though our own tickets are prepaid, they don't include his fare to go underneath as cargo, and he's about ninety pounds too heavy to go in the cabin and sit on my lap.

Diana's nervous, but I'm not too worried. It seems to me that once we explain the situation and that we can have somebody meet us on the other end and pay for him upon arrival, this will all get sorted out. I can't imagine any airline would separate a dog from his people. I'm wrong.

The official at Sabena Airlines could not be more sympathetic. I explain to him about Ubu and about how close we are. How I couldn't have a dog, growing up in Brooklyn, and how Ubu and I have never been separated. How I picked him out of a box of puppies in Sproul Plaza on the Berkeley campus. How he came to every class with me, even the required courses in math and science. How I named him after a play being done in the theater department, *Ubu Roi.* Ubu shows how he can "sit" and "stay" in Flemish, and I begin to think this guy is going to cry. He then pulls from his breast pocket near his heart, two pictures of his own dogs—also Labrador retrievers.

"It's incredible you came to me. I love dogs, as you can see." He hands us the two pictures.

Diana and I ooh and ahh appropriately. I'm about to say something about "your wife's side" but I stop myself.

"That's why it pains me so much to tell you there's nothing I can do to help. Ubu will have to be left behind and kept in a crate. When Sabena receives the money they'll send him over to you."

I try to explain to him that this will not go well. That Ubu will not allow himself to be left behind. There could be an international incident. But the man is unmoved. "Sabena policy"* cannot be overridden.

My head is spinning now as we return to the passenger terminal, where we've set up our mini-campsite. Diana takes out our little Bluet stove and begins to make tea. This is evidently an old Irish custom whenever there's a problem. Put on another cup o' tea. I don't think she even knows she's doing it.

Ubu and I play Frisbee in the corridor. On top of all his other great traits, Ubu is a world-class Frisbee player. He will run thirty, forty yards at full speed chasing the spinning plastic disc and then, at the last second, leap into the air and make the grab, trot back proudly, and drop the Frisbee at my feet. This is a game, by the way, which has no end, and we've been playing on and off now for about three years.

As often happens when we play in a public place, a crowd gathers to watch. This only serves to fire Ubu up, and he's really leaping and twirling, putting on quite a show. This is an international crowd, and I sense Ubu might have Olympic aspirations. I make a note to get him a personal trainer when we get home. If only we could charge people to watch him play . . . and then it hits me. The million-dollar idea. Or, at least the seventy-five-dollar idea, which is what we need to get Ubu on the plane with us.

At first Diana is a little resistant. She has a more finely tuned sense of propriety and dignity that emerges at odd moments, like

---

*Sabena Airlines is no longer in business. Coincidence? I think not.

this one. But eventually the wisdom of my case prevails. Plus, we have no other choice.

We scrounge some cardboard and some magic markers. We make signs in English and French and Spanish that say PLEASE HELP US GET OUR DOG BACK HOME. And Diana, obviously pregnant and a national merit finalist, and Ubu her loving Labrador companion sit down in the middle of the Brussels airport, with an upturned Frisbee in front of them to serve as a collection plate.

Within fifteen minutes, we've exceeded our goal, and people are literally throwing money at us. Tearfully, telling us about the dog they had to leave behind, or the pet they're flying home to see. Ubu handles all the petting and the nuzzling with grace and forbearance. He knows something big is up.

Within a few more minutes, we're a little club of international pet-loving strangers milling about, trying to explain to one another, in different languages and with exaggerated hand gestures, the depth of our affection for animals, and the importance of Ubu getting home safely. People are talking among themselves now, ignoring us. Making new friends. I see one man and woman go off, hand in hand, to have a drink, and my heart gives a little pang.

This is going way too easy and we're all having way too much fun, when out of the corner of my eye, I see him. The angry airport security guard. And he's walking quickly toward us, speaking animatedly into a little walkie-talkie. I'm sure it's just me imagining it, but I believe I can see steam coming out of his ears. Our little pet-lover village disperses with alarming speed, and it's only me, Diana, Ubu, and this guard who are left. I'm thinking to myself two things: One, if he touches Diana, I'll kill him. And two, just don't take the money.

In his cramped basement office, he makes it quite clear that if it was up to him, he would have us executed. Somehow we represent a threat to everything this man believes in. Everything he holds dear. And there is such hatred in his eyes, such malice in his soul, that on some level, it could be considered almost fascinating. But at this moment it is only scary.

Another man comes in, thankfully higher-ranked, and dismisses this guard. The higher-ranked man, though curt, is not maniacal, which is a big step up. He explains the drill. We will stay down here until our flight is called. We will be issued a warning. But we can keep the money. And the three of us can travel back to America, together.

We're left alone in the tiny office now. Our backpacks lean against the wall. Ubu stretches out, a paw touching Diana for comfort. I lean down to pet him. He goes over on his back so I'll be able to do the job more properly. I reach over and take Diana's hand. We exchange a small kiss. She puts her head in my lap. Takes my hand and puts it on her belly. I feel the baby kick. Down the hall, a scratchy radio begins to play Don McLean's "American Pie." It's hard not to be optimistic about the future.

1982

{ c h a p t e r   f o u r }

"We love the show and we want to pick it up."

The voice on the phone, friendly, warm, belongs to Brandon Tartikoff, the brilliant young president of Entertainment at NBC. He's calling to give me good news about *Family Ties,* a pilot I did for his network. I love Brandon, and really respect him. He rescued *Family Ties* from oblivion after CBS turned down the original script.

"Families are dead on TV," Harvey Shephard, the head of CBS Programming, had informed me with great confidence.

"Really? Nobody told me."

"Yeah. Comedies are dead too."

He waved a large sheaf of papers in my direction, which, I could only assume, confirmed this grave diagnosis.

"I don't know," I said, shaking my head. "We kind of like comedy in my house. Especially family comedy."

"Hey, you want to try another network, go ahead."

Back with Brandon on the phone now, still warm and friendly.

"Yeah, we're picking up *Family Ties* on one condition."

"Great. What's that?"

"Replace Michael Fox."

"Excuse me?"

"Just hear him out." Another voice on the conference call now, a little more gravelly, a little more excited, belongs to Gary Nardino, the president of Paramount Television. The last of the great salesmen.

"Replace Michael Fox?" I stammer. "Why?"

"We think it might be better to go with someone taller."

"I didn't realize that was how we cast shows now. By height. Maybe we should get Wilt Chamberlain?"

Brandon, way too classy to come down to my level, continues in a calm, reasoned voice.

"Some of the testing was . . ."

"Testing's bullshit, Brandon. You've said so yourself."

"Yeah, but in this case, I'm not sure I don't agree. Anyway, does this kid have the kind of face that's going to be on a lunch box?"

"I don't know. A thermos, maybe?"

"So, what I'm hearing is, you're open to it and you want to think it over," Nardino chimes in, right out of *Glengarry Glen Ross.* But that's his job, to sell. And he's been a great partner every step of the way.

"I'm not doing this show without Michael Fox."

"We'll get a list of available actors over to you right away," Nardino continues.

"Brandon, if you don't want to put the show on with Michael Fox, don't put the show on. But I'm not doing it without him."

"Should we send the list of actors to the house or to the office?" Nardino wants to know.

I miss Gary Nardino. He's like a pulling left guard, not to be denied. Like Fuzzy Thurston blocking for Jim Taylor. There's a brief silence. Then Brandon speaks.

"Look, if you feel that strongly about it. . . ."

"I do. I really do."

A little more silence, Brandon again. "Why don't we just go with Michael Fox, then."

"Thanks, Brandon."

"But we'll send that list of actors over anyway, OK? In case you change your mind." Nardino, getting in the last word.

Brandon Tartikoff was the best network executive I ever worked with. And he was probably the single most important element in the success of *Family Ties.* Brandon truly loved TV and the process of making TV shows, and he loved the people who made them. And he wasn't afraid to show you that affection. He broke down those walls that seemed to exist, for me anyway, between the "creative" community and the executive suite. He was the first guy more or less my age to run a network, and he made things exciting and fun.

Years later, when *Family Ties* did become a hit show, typical of Brandon, he never "ran" from our 1982 phone call. Never tried to deny he'd said it. Never said he'd been misunderstood. What he said was, "I made a mistake. And I'm glad you didn't listen to me." And when Michael Fox made him a lunch box with Mike's own smiling face on the front, and then put some crow inside for Brandon to eat, Brandon unashamedly put that lunch box on top of his desk. And, it was the first thing you noticed when you walked into Brandon's office.

Brandon was fearless. And he liked to take big swings. Sometimes when you take big swings you strike out. But sometimes you hit a home run.

All successful movies or television shows seem to have one thing in common. They were all turned down, at one time, by someone, somewhere else. Columbia turned down *E.T.* Universal turned down *Star Wars.* ABC turned down *CSI.* Every network turned down *All in the Family.* At the end of the first studio screening of *Breakfast at Tiffany's,* featuring the haunting Henry Mancini song "Moon River," the studio head reportedly stood up and bellowed, "I don't know about this movie, but that fuckin' song is out." And the studio notes on the first screen test of an actor named Fred Astaire: "Can't act. Can't sing. Can dance a little."

The funny thing is, I didn't want Michael Fox at first either. Our talented casting director, Judith Weiner, had discovered a young boy in New York City, just out of high school, no real experience yet, but she thought he'd be perfect for the role of Alex Keaton. His name was Matthew Broderick. When I saw that audition tape, I said what any sane person would say: "Sign him up."

Eventually, that deal fell through, as Matthew decided he wanted to stay in New York and explore opportunities he had in the theater world. Michael Fox was literally the next actor I saw for the role of Alex. And still "on the rebound" from the collapse of the Matthew deal, I wasn't ready yet to fall in love with someone new.

In my defense, and obviously I could do with some defending here, Michael had made a very specific choice in his audition, as to how to play the character of Alex. And it was, in fact, a wrong choice. Mike's such a gifted actor that he always has a wide array of options available to him as to how he's going to approach any role, and in this instance he had chosen to feature what I would call the darker side of Alex Keaton. And to me, in my Paramount office in Hollywood, still in love with Matthew Broderick back in New York, Michael Fox seemed a little harsh, and not so funny that day.

"That was great, thanks, we'll be in touch."

As soon as Michael left, Judith Weiner turned to me, clearly upset, "You're making a terrible mistake. Call him back in here. Ask him to do it again."

"He's not the guy, Judith."

"Yes, he is. He's wonderful."

"He's OK."

"He's wonderful. And, he is absolutely the best actor for this part. There's no one else who's even close."

"Look, Judith, I created the character of Alex Keaton, I think I might have some small idea of who should play him, and it's not Michael J. Fox."

Judith is upset and is giving me the silent treatment. Our relationship is a little bit like a married couple. I love Judith, and this is the third project we've done together.

"Can I see some other actors, please?"

"Fine."

"Are you mad at me, Judith?"

"I'm not mad. I'm disappointed."

It really is like being married.

We proceed to audition about a thousand more actors for the role of Alex Keaton, and every once in a while Judith will say, "Why don't you see Michael Fox again?" And I will say no. It's a game we play once or twice a week, and neither of us seems to be getting tired of it.

In the meantime, another series that Judith has cast for us, *Making the Grade,* will be coming on CBS shortly, and I travel to Washington, D.C., for the Press Tour. The show is extremely well received, and the reviewers are particularly complimentary of the cast Judith has put together, which includes James Naughton, a teenage Emilio Estevez, and the network debut of a young man from Second City, George Wendt. I call Judith to tell her about the raves we're getting for the cast and to thank her for all the hard work she's put in. I've had about fourteen margaritas at this point.

"You're in a good mood."

"I am," I reply, humming "La Bamba" to myself and thinking how much I like margaritas, and how great it is they come in different colors now.

"Will you do me a favor?"

"Anything, señorita! Name it."

"When you come back, will you see Michael Fox again?"

"OK, Judith. I will see Michael Fox again. But only as a favor to you. Because I know he's not the guy."

We set up another casting session, and Michael comes in a second time to read for the role of Alex Keaton.

"Anything you want me to tell you about the character?" I offer.

"No. Just do it better, right."

He smiles sheepishly. Matthew who?

Mike begins to read the scene, and it's immediately obvious, even to me, that he *is* Alex Keaton. Whatever thought process he went through, whatever adjustments he made, he's fabulous. He's funny, smart, charming, just the right amount of bravado, everything I could have dreamed of, in one very cute package. I thank him for his time, he leaves, I turn to Judith Weiner.

"This kid's great. Why didn't you tell me about him?"

We begin filming *Family Ties* on the Paramount lot in Holly-wood. We do the show live in front of a studio audience, and at the start it's difficult to fill those 250 seats on Friday night. Mostly we get the overflow crowd who couldn't get in to see their first-choice show, *Joanie Loves Chachi.* They're shuttled over to us and they are not happy. They sit there, arms folded. "Make us laugh. I dare you."

Well, we try. What choice do we have? After a while, I begin watching the audience as they watch our show. If they're not quite ready to give us a laugh yet, "I don't see Chachi out there," they are beginning to grudgingly give us some smiles, and then as their body language becomes less hostile and their arms unfold, we do begin to get a scattered laugh or two. But what's most interest-ing to me is that when Michael Fox is on stage, the whole audience, unconsciously, leans a little forward. Then, when Michael exits, they unconsciously lean a little back.

We begin to get big "character" laughs for Alex. Then we begin to get laughs just by referring to Alex, even when he's offstage. We get laughs from audiences who don't understand English. *"Donde esta Chachi?"* Somehow people can sense that Michael Fox, in the role of Alex Keaton, is something special.

We've finished four episodes now, and NBC has tested them. Brandon's coming over, and he wants to talk about what they've discovered. He's been our biggest fan and supporter, along with Jeff Sagansky, the vice president, and Jeff Sagansky's secretary, Mare Mazur, who reads all the scripts and loves them.

NBC has been pretty good in terms of not bogging us down each week with a series of nitpicky notes. But occasionally they back-slide. All network notes are the same. There are really only three. And they never vary. Ever. Before the reading of any script I could put them in a sealed envelope. And at the end of that reading, these will be the network notes. I promise.

One: Move the story up. If the murder takes place in scene two, move it up to scene one. If it already takes place in scene one, move it up to the main title. If it's in the main title now, move it up to the song. Just move it up.

Two: Hang a lantern on it. This means make your main story point so startlingly obvious, so starkly black and white, that it will be robbed of all the shading and complexity and ambiguity that make characters, and life, interesting and compelling. This idea dates back to Elizabethan times, I believe, when it was known as "hangeth a lantern" and is always painful and embarrassing and uninteresting when fully realized.

Three: Raise the stakes. For some reason, every episode must have monumental consequences for all the main characters. Leaving them distraught, bereft, yet somehow enlightened.

Never mind that the most successful TV comedy of all time, *Seinfeld,* rarely ever even had a story to move up. Didn't shine a flashlight, let alone hang a lantern, on anything. And had no stakes whatsoever to be raised.

Brandon sits across from me now in my Paramount office, and he gets right to it.

"You've got lightning in a bottle here with Michael Fox."

He hands me some pages that contain a summary of all the research they've done so far. Turns out even people who don't like the show like Mike. For the people who do like the show, they can't get enough of Mike. It cuts across all ages and gender categories. NBC would like the emphasis of the show to be more on him now. More on the kids.

"I'm not telling you what to do creatively," Brandon went on. "But I just thought you should see this."

That was typical of Brandon and one of the traits that made him such a great network executive. The best studio heads I've worked with—Grant Tinker, Frank Mancuso, Jeffrey Katzenberg, Alan Horn—all have that same manner and style. At the beginning of any "creative" discussion with Alan Horn, he will say, "At the end of this meeting, you will do exactly what you want to do. I'll support you one hundred percent and I'll never revisit these issues again. But here's what I think."

Alan, Jeffrey, Grant, Brandon, Frank—put them in charge of any type of business, and within three years, that business will be preeminent in that particular industry. In the end, you don't want to fail because you don't want to betray the trust they have in you.

Brandon then proceeds to offer one more specific piece of advice for me to consider. And it would have enormous impact on the way I would approach the making of *Family Ties*.

"There are three things that have to happen for a family show to succeed on television," he tells me. "First, the audience has to begin to watch because they recognize themselves in that TV family. Second, they continue to watch because, on some level, they want to be a part of that family. And third, and this is where you can really make your connection deep and lasting, they will watch because they believe they can learn how to be a better family."

"Sounds like a lot for a half-hour show." I laugh.

1969

{ c h a p t e r   f i v e }

*D*iana and I have seen each other a few more times since the Cloisters. One night I call her around midnight.

"What are you doin' tonight?"—trying to be very cool and show her how late I can stay up.

"I haven't decided yet. I might fly to Paris"—being much cooler than me in her response.

We go to the Village Gate that night to see B.B. King. We are, of course, put in the front row by my "colleagues" there. Unending free drinks. Little green pills that can make a person very happy for about thirty-six hours. If not happy, at least active.

After the show I walk Diana back to her apartment on Waverly Place. We stop in at Chumley's, an after-hours bar on Bedford Street, for a very late night, or very early morning, drink, depending on how you want to look at it. One of the great things about working in the Village is the special treatment you get at all the Village bars and nightclubs. Everyone wants to be nice to me and give me free drinks so, when they come to the Village Gate, I'll be nice to them and give them free drinks. Makes for fun nights.

We say good night outside on the street in front of Diana's apartment. She's really tired and has a flight to Spain in the afternoon. And given the effect of the pills I've taken, I want to get back to my apartment anyway, and alphabetize my record collection. Maybe reupholster the furniture.

That B.B. King night was great. One we will always remember. But between her flying around the world and me flying around Greenwich Village, we can't seem to consistently connect. Diana has flatly rejected my theory that sleeping together very early in a relationship is a great way to get to know someone. And I fear that's created some distance between us.

I'm touring the South as an actor in a traveling dinner-theater production of *Under the Yum Yum Tree.* Greensboro, Shreveport, Hot Springs, towns like that. Diana's flying with Pan Am. London, Madrid, Rome, towns like that. And yet I can't convince her to give that up and come be with me in Arkansas.

This is the third tour I've done with this particular group, the Country Dinner Theatre. You usually go out for three months at a time to unsuspecting hamlets on their circuit. The crowd is usually sleepy from overeating, and pretty drunk by the time the show starts. Which, in the case of this show, is not a bad idea. The Playbill says "Broadway Cast," not because it's true but because we were cast out of a building at 1697 Broadway. Which gives you a good idea of who you're dealing with here.

I never had any actual interest in acting. I was just trying to meet girls. Acting school seemed like a good place to start, so I signed up for a class at the HB Studio, on Bank Street. After the first class, I went up to the teacher and thanked him.

"That was great. I think I got it."

"Got what?"

"The acting thing. I learned a lot tonight. I think I'm ready."

"After one class? People study acting their whole life."

"You're kidding. I mean, it's just pretend, right?"

He may still be laughing.

I went to the library to begin work on my résumé. First I researched plays that had opened and closed quickly in the last few years, to see which ones I might have been in. Then I threw in some bit parts in John Cassavetes movies, which were a safe bet, since so many were unreleased and you could always say your scene got cut.

Finally, I came up with some "representative roles," which I felt were roles I could have played if anyone had actually asked me to play them. And pretty soon I had a résumé that made me look like a young guy starting out, which I was. And a young guy with a modicum of talent, which I was not.

I get a copy of *Back Stage* and begin making the rounds of casting directors, open "cattle calls," theatrical agents, and producers. Since I have no real vested interest in being an actor, this part of the process is not particularly painful for me. I like walking around the city meeting people. "Just dropping off a picture and a résumé." I'd smile. And I actually felt like I was in show business. Talk about pretend.

At the end of one of the longer days, I was making my way up a steep flight of stairs at 1697 Broadway, getting ready to drop off my picture and résumé at the Country Dinner Theatre office and then head back down to the Village Gate and work that night. I had no way of knowing it, but at that precise moment, the producer was on the phone with the theater owner in Marietta, Georgia, and they had just fired the leading man in the show they were doing down there, *Avanti,* by Samuel Taylor. Basically, the guy back in Georgia was in a panic screaming, "I need somebody. Anybody. Just send me the first shmuck who walks through the door."

I peek my head in. "You guys have anything?"

I arrive in Marietta, Georgia, and meet with the director, Jay Feldman, who, even by musical-comedy standards, may be a little too gay. I'm to work with him in the afternoons, while observing the show in the evening. And in six days, I will open in the lead role, when the show moves to Roanoke, Virginia.

We begin rehearsing, just me and Jay at this point, and after a few moments it becomes clear to him.

"You've never acted, have you?"

"Technically no. That's right."

"Never, ever?"

"I was in *Oklahoma,* at Camp Oquago."

I had never witnessed a person having an actual panic attack, so I didn't recognize the early warning signs. Jay just kept screaming, "Never acted. He's never acted. I trained at Yale. And they've sent me someone who has never acted."

I tried to point out the positives.

"Look, I'm here. I speak English. These are my original teeth."

"You've never acted!"

"Stop saying that. You're making me nervous."

"But it's true. My good God in heaven, it's true."

"C'mon, you have to work with me. I'm all you've got. I'm a fast learner. I'm not going to hurt anybody. And I'll do whatever you tell me without asking any questions."

That last part appealed to the director in him, and for the first time he began to focus and resumed almost normal breathing. He'd also stopped crying now, which was helpful.

"All right, let's start at the top, then. You enter stage left."

I went off and came on.

"That's stage right."

I went back off, came out from the other side. "Better. That is, in fact, stage right. Well done."

After coming to grips with what had been thrust upon him, Jay Feldman turned out to be an excellent director. He was always patient with me personally. Inventive and enthusiastic about the material. Energetic and always willing to "try it one more time."

We are scheduled to go on in twenty-four hours now, and at this point, I think, *robotlike* most captures the quality I'm bringing to the role. Jay is still my cheerleader. "We've come a long way," he points out, generously not mentioning how far we still have to go.

The reviewers in Roanoke are not kind. While panning the show in general, they single me out in particular: "Completely wooden," "sticklike." I'm sensing a forest theme here. And my favorite: "This is an amateur production but it shines compared to the performance of . . ."

I'm actually clipping these reviews out and putting them in my book. Because I know what these people don't—I've never acted. I didn't hurt anybody. I didn't knock over any scenery. The more subtle aspects of my performance will have to wait to emerge.

We do eight shows a week. Jay works with me every afternoon. I'm really touched and impressed by his commitment. We become friends. I learn way too much about his childhood and love life. Both unhappy. I tell him about my childhood. The cocoon of love and affection that was our neighborhood in Brooklyn. Sharing a room with my older brother, whom I idolized. Who never diminished me or made me feel small. About my parents, who offered only encouragement and respect. He thinks I'm making it up.

One night, after the show, we go out to a local diner. It's me, Jay, a couple of the more flamboyant cast members. Actually, they were all flamboyant cast members. And as we noisily enter, loud colorful scarves dramatically flipped over slender shoulders, several burly guys at the counter jerk their heads up from their coffee as we walk by, and you can see the progression in their thought process: Jew, fag, dyke, two more Jews, another fag. They're not far off the mark here, by the way.

Kenny Pickens, who could make Truman Capote look like Rocky Marciano, shivered nervously in our booth.

"My God, they look like they could eat us alive."

"You'd like that, wouldn't you, Kenny?" from Jay.

"Fellas, please," from me.

"I feel like Rita Hayworth, in *Blood and Sand,*" more from Kenny.

"Love *Blood and Sand.* Love Tyrone Power," from Jay.

"Love the tight pants with the little appliqué. . . ."

"Guys, seriously."

I look over at the counter, at the men in overalls and baseball caps who are glaring at us, and my first thought, shamefully, is, "I'm not like these guys, you're making a mistake. I played basketball in Madison Square Garden. I had my high-school scoring record. Third team all-city in the *Post* in 1962, look it up." And I realize too, shamefully, that a couple of years earlier, I could have very easily been sitting on that other side of the room staring warily at this group of very different-looking people. And been comfortable there. I hear one guy mutter, "Fuckin' theater," and the other guys nod, and fortunately they just go back to their coffee and their pie.

In my memory, I put my arm around Jay and give him a hug. But I'm sure I could not have been that thoughtful. Or that brave.

I get hired three more times by the Country Dinner Theatre Company to go out on tours. Once, in *The Odd Couple,* where I'm criminally miscast as Murray the Cop, and twice more in reprises of *Yum Yum Tree.* Why this show needs to be reprised, God only knows, but it is a big fan favorite with hard-drinking Southerners, of whom there seems to be no shortage.

We're winding down this particular production in Hot Springs, Arkansas, and I have a decision to make about where to go from here. My friend Peter has moved out to Sausalito, California, and wants me to come out and stay with him. I've been sending him my paychecks to hold, and right now he's got about $2,400 of mine, which I figure should last me about eleven years. Also, I know that Diana has moved back to Northern California and is living across the bay, in Oakland.

Pete's house is high up in the hills with a great view of the town of Sausalito below. He is recently married, to Gretchen, also a stewardess. And, while not thrilled to have me living with them, Gretchen's cordial in an ice-cold, Teutonic sort of way. Pete's the perfect host, except for one minor detail: He has gambled and lost all the money I have sent him.

Curiously, this does not upset me. I love Pete, and I know in his own mind he actually thought he was doing me a favor. That he was going to double my money for me and maybe make a little for himself. And he was shocked when it did not turn out that way. This is very Brooklyn.

Pete is also curiously not upset by this turn of events and promises me I'll get all my money back, which I never doubt for a moment. Also, I'm going to get to live with him and Gretchen rent free, and I'll have the run of the house and use of the car. He offers his bedroom, saying he and Gretchen will sleep out on the couch in the living room. I can tell by the various shades of red she's turning that Pete has not discussed this with her. This seems like more than I need; the couch will be fine.

Pete promises that if I want to bring someone home though, a girl say, that he and Gretchen will vacate the premises, and I can use their bedroom. Again, this clearly has not been a joint decision. Pete and Gretchen are no longer together, by the way.

I love Sausalito. This is my first time in Northern California, and I can't believe how beautiful it is. In the morning, after Pete and Gretchen have gone off to work, I sit out on the deck and read the paper. The *San Francisco Chronicle,* in a brilliant stroke, prints the sports section in green so you don't have to waste time searching through the rest of the paper to find it. In the afternoon I walk down into town and read Henry Miller on the promenade, hoping to be mistaken for someone more intellectual and artistic than I am.

One day, Pete comes home and tells me he received a call at work from Diana. She's having a party Friday night and invited him and Gretchen and said she heard I was in town and I could come with them if I wanted. I told Pete I definitely did want to go, and furthermore, I was going to pack my bag, because I wouldn't be coming back. I was certain Diana was going to ask me to move in with her. Pete looked at me like I was crazy.

"This is a beautiful, intelligent, well-traveled girl who can have any guy she wants. Why is she going to ask you to move in with her?"

I couldn't answer that question either, but still I had a feeling I was right.

The party was nice. I thought there were too many good-looking guys there, but that was just my opinion. Diana was more beautiful than I remembered, if that was possible. She had heard about my "move" out to California.

"Won't you miss the Cloisters?" she wanted to know.

"I'll go back on weekends."

That got a little smile from her. Not bad for a C-plus joke attempt. Beautiful *and* generous. Music came on, and we began to dance. After a brief discussion about who was going to lead, Diana having spent way too many years in Catholic girls' schools, we settled in and began to move across the floor. Neither one of us could dance very well, and I found that very comforting. I loved how fluidly inept we were, elbows flying, knees bending, laughing and laughing and then laughing some more.

At the end of the night the crowd thinned and Diana asked me if I wanted to stay the night.

"I'll get my bag."

She didn't hit me, which I thought was a nice gesture. She may have even smiled. I went down with Pete to his car. We said an emotional good-bye. I walked back up the stairs to Diana's apartment that night, I stepped inside, and I would stay for the rest of my life.

{chapter six}

*D*iana and I have been living together for five months now, and I think I may be falling in love with her. It's hard for me to tell. I've always liked best the kind of relationships where not much is asked of me. As for actual feelings, I haven't spent a lot of time trying to locate mine. Never needed them before.

In high school, where I fear I may have peaked, I was captain of the basketball team, and my girlfriend was captain of the cheerleaders. She was very sweet. Very smart. The prettiest girl in the school. I don't remember if we ever even really wanted to go out with each other. It seemed like we were just supposed to.

I had one other serious girlfriend in high school. The co-captain of the cheerleaders. Beautiful. Incredibly smart. She went on to become a psychologist with a successful practice in Chicago. Many years later, when we were both in our early fifties, we met for dinner in New York City. We exchanged pictures of our beloveds. Of our children. Our pets. She was as sweet and charming as I remembered.

"Do you know that you just stopped talking to me one day?" she asked.

"I don't remember."

"I never knew what I did. Or what I said. But you just stopped talking to me. It really hurt my feelings."

As a trained therapist, she can locate her feelings, so I'm at a distinct disadvantage here, but I figure I may as well give it a try.

"OK, this is not an excuse, it's barely an explanation, and maybe I'm giving myself too much credit for having any insight into this, but I think, at some point, I must have come to believe you might really like me. And that probably scared the hell out of me. That was the only way I could deal with it, I guess. Maybe that's it. And I'm sorry."

While pointing out that this might be just a little self-serving on my part (these therapists see right through you), we agree that a crème brûlée and two more brandies might allow us to put this all behind us.

I have a question for her now, and it is one I've been thinking about for a while. In our neighborhood, there were a lot of really smart, really lovely girls, like her. And a lot of narrow, sports-obsessed, "guys-only" guys like me. Guys who had girlfriends but clearly weren't serious about it. Or in any way willing to deal with these girls as actual, separate, independent individuals. In our neighborhood, the bond between the guys was always going to be so much stronger than any bond between a boy person and a girl person.

"You girls were obviously so far above us. So much more evolved. Why did you put up with guys like us?"

She looked at me for a moment.

"You were all we had."

While that didn't do much for my self-esteem, and I'm thinking I might have to go into therapy myself now, I thank her for solving that part of the puzzle for me.

Throughout the 1960s I continued this pattern of shallow "don't ask, don't tell me anything about yourself, or about your feelings, and I won't burden you with any of mine, and we can have fun until it looks as though one of us might, actually, care about the other, and that will be the signal that it's time for me to go" kind of behavior.

This was the era of "if you can't be with the one you love, love the one you're with," and a lot of young people found it hard to argue with that kind of logic. There was also the larger political context you could always call on for support. The importance of rethinking all the bourgeois conventions that seemed stifling and phony. The liberating power of "free love."

"Look, I'm tired too, and I don't really want to have sex with you, either. But, I think we owe it to the movement."

"Oh?"

"This is bigger than just me and you and what we might, or might not, want to do on any one particular night. Our sleeping together is actually connected to a much larger political agenda."

"Oh?"

"It's like it's not even sex, really. It's a blow for freedom. We are soldiers in a grand alliance. And we can't let down our brothers and sisters."

"You're fuckin' kidding me, right?"

OK, sometimes it didn't work. But a lot of times, surprisingly, it did.

Now, this time around, with Diana, everything seems different. When she's away on a trip, I really miss her. I'm lonely. I nap a lot. My appetite's still good, thank God. And, my color is OK. These being the two constant markers of good health among Jews. But I'm otherwise listless and not engaged. The world's in black and white. When she returns, my life goes back to Technicolor.

On a day that Diana's going to be returning from a trip, I wake up early, in anticipation. I tidy up. I've never tidied up before. I even make the bed and put back those fluffy pillows, which I hate, and I've stored in the closet while she's been away. I really don't like the fluffy pillows. It's the one thing that's not going right for us. I make a note to bring this up at some future moment, when we're further along in our relationship, and I'm feeling more secure. Still waiting for the right moment, by the way.

Diana comes over to the window where I'm sitting. Hands me a copy of the *Berkeley Barb.* Points to an advertisement at the bottom of the page. GO HOME FREE FOR CHRISTMAS, it reads.

"What do you think?" she smiles. "Could be fun, huh?"

It seems that the Hertz corporation, this summer of love*, has found itself with a glut of big moving trucks, which have been left out here in San Francisco. Hertz needs to get those trucks back to New York City. And if you drive one of these trucks back East for them, Hertz will pay all gas and tolls along the way.

I hand the paper back to her, "Trip to New York? We should think about it."

"I think we should just go."

"What about work? Don't you have a flight coming up?"

"I quit. I don't want to work anymore. I just want to be with you."

"Quit work? Just like that? Is that a wise move?"

I'm sounding incredibly like my father now and totally missing the impact of the rather large romantic gesture Diana has just tossed out. I try to recover.

"We should call Hertz. See if they have any trucks left."

"We can leave tomorrow."

I look at her smiling, happy, completely beautiful face.

"Sounds good to me."

She kisses me.

"Hey, Diana, you know those fluffy pillows we have on the bed?"

"Sure, I love those pillows. What about them?"

"Nothing. Just . . . we should get some more."

We arrive at the Hertz truck center, which is in a very industrial part of South San Francisco. After we fill out all the forms, we're given the keys to the largest vehicle I've ever seen. A big, yellow monster of a truck.

"You ever drive one of these before?" the Hertz guys asks.

"Yeah, my aunt Esther had one."

---

*The actual "summer of love" was 1967, but the effects were still lingering.

He gives me a courtesy laugh. Cautions us about always using both the mirrors. Pulling out slowly into traffic. Don't have to worry about speed. The motor has a "governor." It won't go over 60 mph. He gives us a map with the suggested, approved route—I-80 through Utah, Nevada, and Wyoming. The Northern passage. It should take eight to ten days to make the trip.

"What happens if it takes us longer than ten days to get to New York?"

He gives me the universal, paid-by-the-hour working man's "like I could give a shit" look. And, we pull out of the Hertz lot and immediately head south to pick up the I-10, which will take us to New Orleans, which Diana thinks will be a great place for us to spend Christmas.

"It's going to be our first Christmas together," she tells me. "I want it to be special."

"Let's hope the Hertz people feel the same way."

Over the next few days we barrel along through California into Arizona, then into New Mexico, and into Texas. I have really, really long hair, which I try to keep contained underneath a baseball cap, but I'm still a little leery about moving through this part of the country. I'm not exactly an Okie from Muskogee. But my fears are unfounded. I don't know if it's the big yellow truck, or the holiday season, or the unseasonably mild weather, but everyone we meet along the way is gracious and helpful.

We do have one bad moment, though, when we stop off for coffee at a little place outside of Seguin, Texas. The sign reading HOME-MADE DONUTS — FRESH AND PRETTY was not one we could resist, and we pulled into the parking lot in front of the cute little bungalow, with a front porch and a screen door. I'm thinking two dozen of whatever they have and we can call it lunch and dinner. Diana's right there with me. On top of everything else, she's got a healthy appetite, thank God. And, her color's good too.

As we bound up the steps, a man appears in the doorway, barring our way. He's standing inside, and he's cradling something in his arms. It's hard to see through the screen door, and I'm hoping I'm mistaken, but it looks something like a shotgun.

"Are you guys hippies?" he drawls, accenting the word "hippies" in a manner that lets you know he's not a fan, and may have read the *Time* magazine piece with Charles Manson on the cover. Or more likely, had someone read it to him.

"Hippies?" I laughed. "I don't know. What are they?"

Diana gives the guy her best "aisle or window" smile.

"We'd just like some pretty doughnuts. Maybe coffee to go with it."

We start to go up one more step and he pushes the screen door open a notch. And yes, it is a shotgun, we can both clearly see that now.

"I don't want you in my place."

We look at each other. We look at the shotgun. We turn and walk back to the truck. I take Diana's hand.

"Maybe if he knew your SAT scores."

That night we make it to the outskirts of Beaumont and pull into a campsite to sleep. We open up the back of the truck, unroll the sleeping bags, and climb in. We leave the huge rear sliding door open, and we can see the stars twinkling high above the Texas plains.

Diana tells me about Christmas past in her house. Her dad's meticulous tree-trimming ritual, with the strict limits on the amount of tinsel to be used, each strand having to be placed by hand. The heirloom bubble-lights, which have survived moves from New Mexico, to Colorado, to Maryland, back to New Mexico, and then over to California. Of caroling and eggnog and midnight mass. Of the squeals of delight at the new bike or new electric train set that would be wrapped, in a bow, underneath the tree.

I explain to her how I could never have electric trains as a kid growing up. Too dangerous. Could start a fire. Or the train could jump off the track and take an eye out. Not that anyone in my family could ever assemble an electric train set, but that was beside the point.

My cousin Richard had electric trains, and when Stanley and I went over there we'd get to play with them for hours. Richard went on to become a doctor, and I always felt there was some connection between his having his own electric trains and his medical degree.

Diana laughs, but there's a small sadness in her tonight. This will be the first Christmas she won't be with her family. They didn't want me there. So it was either them or me. And she made her choice. I think I would have chosen them, but I don't feel right pointing that out now.

I don't know what to do to help make this more festive. Christmas in our house was decidedly less dramatic. We were willing to go as far as watching the Perry Como Christmas special, but when Perry started to talk about the baby Jesus, there would be a lot of coughing, followed by somebody saying, "What's on the other channel?"

The temperature's dropping rapidly now, and we scrunch up closer together in our sleeping bags. We lie there in silence, watching the star show. One of the great things about Diana is how she can just enjoy these silent moments. She's not like most girls, who have to ask you every two minutes, "What're you thinking about?" A question most guys are completely unprepared to answer.

"What're you thinking about?" she asks softly.

I try, desperately, to come up with the name of a poet, any poet, which I feel would be impressive, maybe even sexy, although it's really cold now and I don't know if two people can even fit in these sleeping bags. Still, you don't want to close any doors prematurely. What about that guy with the girl's name, who wrote about trees? Or the guy who wrote "Casey at the Bat?" Is that a poem or a limerick?

"Just enjoying the night," I whisper. "It's like I have so many different thoughts that I don't have any," and even as I'm saying it, I'm thinking to myself, *What can that possibly mean?*

"I know exactly how you feel," Diana answers softly. She snuggles even closer, and I move one step further down the path to being hopelessly in love.

1982

{chapter seven}

The process of doing a half-hour, multicamera television show in front of a live audience means putting on a new twenty-three-minute play each week. And while this format may have been invented for Lucille Ball, there's one other person on this earth who was born to thrive in this form, and that is Michael J. Fox.

Michael inhales this process, redefines it, makes it his own. He's never defensive. Loves last-minute changes. Always trying to make it better. He lives for the show in front of the audience on Friday night. And, he's pretty damn funny.

Our work week begins on Monday morning with the "table read" of that week's script. The goal in this process of read, rehearse, and rewrite is to get everyone to peak at the same time, in front of that audience when those cameras are rolling.

After each run-through we all sit around the table in the Keaton kitchen and talk about the script. I talk about what we were trying to do, from a writing point of view. What I thought was successful. What I thought didn't work. Then I go around the table and ask each actor specifically what was working for them. What wasn't. Where they were uncomfortable.

Mike Fox's responses are always instinctive. A good hitter trying to find the right bat. A golfer reaching for the proper club. Michael Gross, very analytical, is always probing in a classic, theatrical thrust—interested in subtext, interested in motivation. Meredith

Baxter, trained in one-hour dramas, is primarily interested in the logic of her behavior. Always after the reason and justification for the event.

So, if during a scene around the kitchen table, for example, a bowl of shrimp was suddenly put down, Michael Gross would say, "Why only shrimp?" Meredith Baxter would say, "Do I like shrimp?" And Mike Fox would say, "Are those the funniest shrimp we could get?"

We're in a kind of crossover period in TV at the moment, where some of the earlier directors, who were gifted technical practitioners, are finding themselves less comfortable dealing with the more emotional storytelling style we're developing. So I go out into the theatre world to find directors who are able to maintain a dialogue with our cast on a level that their talent demands.

I go to see a performance of a Pinter play, *Betrayal,* directed by Sam Weisman, an actor turned director. This is the first Pinter play I've ever actually understood, let alone enjoyed. I figure if Sam can do this with Pinter, he's certainly not going to have any problem with *Family Ties.* Sam comes on board to become a trusted partner, and we begin a collaboration that will last for more than twenty years.

At South Coast Repertory, I find a talented young woman, Lee Shallat. From Brown University we get John Pasquin. Also from Brown, and a former actor on *Newhart,* we get Will Mackenzie. Along with Asaad Kelada, who directed the pilot, I now have a nucleus of really talented and smart collaborators.

I encourage the directors to be advocates for the actors. To always bring back to me the reality of what's happening on that stage. From Sam Weisman I learn a valuable concept, "actability." He'll come back and say, "Gary, it's really funny. But it can't be acted. There's no entry point for an actor to come into the scene." Our actors are too good to just stand around and hurl jokes, and we always try to provide the emotional context for them to do their work.

In one script, however, early on, there's a joke for Mike Fox that's indefensible from any logic point of view. But I think it could be a big laugh, and I've left it in, knowing that if Mike asks "Why?" or "Would I?" I'll have to cut it.

I'm up all night trying to think of what I'll say to this young guy, who trusts me, that will allow this joke to stay in the script. I come up with some justification. It's flimsy and weak and obviously fake, but at least it's something. I see Mike on set the next day.

"Hey, Mike, you know that joke in the B scene?"

Mike puts up a hand.

"I'll find a reason, don't worry. It's really funny. I'll make it work."

He gives me a little love tap on the shoulder and goes off. This could be a fun seven years, I'm thinking.

The writing staff on the pilot episode was me, Lloyd Garver, a talented and funny *Newhart* veteran, and Michael Weithorn, a young man who was a teacher at the Brentwood School when we met. He'd written a spec *Barney Miller* I thought was great, and fifteen minutes into our meeting, I said, "Stop, you're hired. I love you."

Michael will go on to create the hit show *King of Queens,* but this is his first job in show business. And, in truth, in those early episodes of *Family Ties,* Michael had a much keener insight into the character of Alex Keaton than I did. And it's hard to imagine the show succeeding without Michael Weithorn's contribution.

After the pilot, we added one other writer, Ruth Bennett. Ruth had written a spec *M*A*S*H* I'd read and thought was brilliant. But when I called her agent to set up a meeting with her, he told me Ruth wasn't in America anymore. She was living on a kibbutz in Israel. So if I was going to hire her, I'd have to do it without us ever meeting. I reread her spec *M*A*S*H* and decided I didn't need to have a meeting. There was no way I wasn't going to love the person who wrote that.

Ruth said when her agent called her in Israel, it was surreal. She had just returned from a day in the fields picking oranges. And when she got on the phone, he told her to come back to L.A. immediately and go to work on this new TV show, *Family Ties.* I pictured kibbutzniks all over Israel receiving calls to come to Hollywood as they got off their tractors.

"Yitzhak, you're on *A-Team*. Mordechai, *Hill Street Blues*, Avram, *Fall Guy*, let's go."

In the middle of that first year, Michael Weithorn creates the character of Elyse's younger brother, Ned, a business genius who's Alex's idol. And he has a young actor in mind to play that role— Tom Hanks. Tom had starred in a short-lived ABC show, *Bosom Buddies*, and he has a movie coming out soon, *Splash*, for which there are high hopes. But we're still able to sign him to do three shows for us at a fairly reasonable rate.

For Mike Fox, it was love at first sight. After the initial reading of the script, Mike came back to the writers' room and was barely able to keep from floating up to the ceiling, he was so excited.

"I love this guy. I love him."

He wasn't going to get an argument from any of us.

"I need to be in a scene with him. Just me and him. Give him all the jokes, I don't care. I just want to be on stage with that guy, alone. Just me and him. I don't need any lines. Please, Gary, please."

Between filming the first episode with Tom and beginning to film the second about two months later, *Splash* came out in theaters, and it was a huge hit, catapulting Tom Hanks into the ranks of legitimate movie stars. We immediately receive a call from Tom's agent, basically reneging on our agreement.* There's almost no chance that he'll do the agreed-upon *Family Ties* episodes, we're told, and if he were to do them, it would have to be for at least ten times the originally agreed-upon price.

A day or two later the phone rings in my office, and it's Tom Hanks.

"Have these guys been bustin' your balls?" Tom wants to know, using the legal terminology for what's been going on here.

"A little bit," I have to admit.

---

*No longer Tom's agent.

"Listen, man, I loved working with you guys. I love Mike Fox. Anytime, anywhere. At the original price, OK?"

"You drive a hard bargain, Tom. But OK."

Now, when Tom comes back again, Mike gets his wish. In an episode "Say Uncle," written by Ruth Bennett, the last scene in the first act finds Tom Hanks and Michael J. Fox alone onstage.

Tom, as Uncle Ned, an alcoholic, unable and unwilling to face his disease, is rummaging through the late night kitchen, looking for something to drink. Anything. There he comes face-to-face with the adoration and admiration of his young nephew. And is forced to confront the demons threatening to overwhelm him.

There's great integrity to the work of both men. And they both play the honest middle very well. They don't need to step outside themselves and "frame" the comedy. Take on a funny persona. In effect saying to the audience, "Here comes the funny part." They don't "ask for the laugh." They don't "cry" for their character. They stay connected to the material, whatever "truth" they're finding there, and they let the audience decide whether they want to laugh or not.

I was so proud and happy for Mike that night. He did not, in fact, have many jokes in that scene. Didn't actually have a lot of lines. But it was his behavior that informed the scene and allowed it to happen. Allowed us to see Ned's disintegration through his eyes. When Ned harshly pushed Alex away, the audience gasped. And the pain and hurt on Alex's face was their pain. And when the scene ended you could hear a pin drop, then huge applause.

Twenty-five years later, I can still see it clearly in my mind's eye. Still call up that shiver of excitement on the back of my neck, watching these two extremely talented young actors, soon to become household names and beloved stars. And I could tell watching them, how much respect they had for each other. And how much they enjoyed playing one-on-one out there.

After we had cast Mike as Alex, after Judith Weiner finally agreed to let me see him a second time, we actually had trouble closing the deal. Not because Mike wanted more money but because his agent,

Bob Gersh, couldn't locate him. It seems Mike couldn't afford a phone, and he was using a Pioneer Chicken outlet up on Highland Avenue as his "office." Bob had no choice but to wait for Mike to show up at Pioneer, order a bucket of wings, and check in with him.

Back then, Mike had a big round sectional couch in his living room, and he was selling off sections of the couch one by one to stay alive. I think he was down to a cushion and a half. He told me later that, had he not gotten the part of Alex Keaton, he was going to give up and quit. Go back to Canada.

I will watch Michael Fox go from phoneless furniture salesman to one of the biggest stars in show business. And one day, with *Back to the Future* and *Family Ties*, he will find himself the star of a number-one movie and a number-one television show. Something that had never happened before.

In our seven years together on *Family Ties,* Michael will never miss one day of work holding out for more money. He'll never ask to have his dressing room enlarged or his parking spot improved. Never ask to have his billing changed from third place, where it was in the original pilot. And he will make stage 24 at Paramount Studios an awfully exciting place to come to work each day.

1972

{chapter eight}

We're seated in the kitchen of my brother's house in Staten Island, having just flown in from Brussels the day before. Stanley and my sister-in-law, Starr, who's really more like my sister, have rolled out the welcome mat for us. They've even made up a special dog bed for Ubu, which they've set up out in the garage. There's really no chance of him sleeping in the garage unless we're out there sleeping with him, but no need to get into that quite yet.

Stanley's got the barbeque set up outside, and evidently he's become quite the "grill king" while we've been abroad. Ubu keeps running out there to check on how the meat is coming. He's never seen an actual barbeque before, and he's very excited. He keeps trying to drag me out there, as if to say, "We should get one of these."

From time to time I see Stan look over at me as if he's about to ask a question, then think better of it. I know he and Starr are both worried about me and Diana. They've always been there for us. Sent money. Bailed us out of some sticky situations. Never judgmental. But I can tell they want to know what our plans are. How we're going to take care of the baby. How we're going to earn a living. These are all good questions, and I'd like to know the answers myself.

My brother seems really happy. Starr's his junior-high-school girlfriend. Beautiful, sweet, loves my brother. Two adorable little daughters. The whole package. At the moment Stan's holding down five separate jobs. His regular teaching job from eight to three, the after-school center from three to six, and then the night center from seven to nine. On weekends he teaches driver's ed. And in the summer he's the head counselor at Trail's End Camp, which he and Starr will one day own.

Stan was always a great worker. Like my father. Wherever they were hired, whatever job they were being paid to do, they were always the favorite employee. The ones that all the other workers looked up to. I got fired from every job I ever had.

One summer Stanley got me a job at the Holiday Hotel in the Catskills, where he was the head busboy and in charge of the dining room. He was starting NYU that fall, and during the summer he would make his college tuition. I was going to be helping out with the concession. Providing tea and coffee for the card players. Bringing soda and candy to the pool.

One small structural problem with that plan. The pool was placed at the top of a very steep hill. The clientele at the Holiday Hotel averaged eighty-three years of age, and there was literally not one guest who could make it up that hill and survive to swim in the pool.

The first day I did as I was told and carried an incredibly heavy pail of sodas up there, in case, miraculously, someone did survive the walk up and might need a ginger ale, instead of what they'd really need, which was CPR. I sat there all day next to my pail of sodas. No one came. I went back up a second day and, again, it was just me and the pail. I did this one more day, and then on the fourth day I said no. This is pointless. I ask what particular hotel guest they had in mind who could survive this Bataan Death March up to the pool and then be so suave and debonair as to actually ask for a soda at that point, rather than an ambulance. I was fired on the spot.

My father explained the work world to me.

"They're paying you. You have to do what they say."

I point out that it made no sense. It was a crazy waste of time to send me up there with those sodas. Dad explained the work world once again.

"They're paying you. You have to do what they say."

During Christmas breaks while I was in college, my father got me on at the post office as a temp. You had to wear a little button that said 89 DAY TEMP. It was bright green and shiny and really helpful if you wanted to pick up girls. Anyway, the job paid over four bucks an hour, and my dad had to call in a lot of favors to get me that position.

We worked out of an almost incomprehensibly ugly building off the Gowanus Expressway. I worked the four to midnight shift. I would punch in at four, and, after working about six hours, I would check the clock. It was 4:10.

The work was bone-crushingly boring. I could feel the marrow being sucked out of my brain as I dragged bags of junk mail across the floor and put them in their proper bins. To keep my spirits up, I would sometimes see if I could put a bag of mail in the bin going to the absolute farthest point away from its actual destination.

After I finished my third season at the post office, I vowed to myself never to go in that building again. My dad said OK, but they were holding my last check there for me, and I had to go in to pick it up.

"I can't do that."

"Why not?"

"I vowed never to go in that building again," I told him, sensing that this, most likely, would not be perceived as a valid argument.

"But they have your check."

"I know."

"I can't pick it up for you. You have to sign for it yourself."

"I vowed never to go in that building."

"They have your check."

"I vowed."

My father took a long look at me and shook his head.

"Where did you come from?"

I couldn't answer that. But I knew I was never going back inside that building.

Stan and Starr have invited a lot of my old high-school friends over today. Mostly our 1962 Lafayette basketball team. These guys, almost to a man, have become phys-ed teachers. That was the highest male role model you could aspire to in our neighborhood. And they will go on to very successful careers coaching, affecting the lives of generations of young people with whom they come in contact.

The talk quickly turns to the championship game we lost to Wingate in Madison Square Garden in 1962. We lost by one point on a questionable foul call against Freddie Grasso as the clock expired. The wound, a mere decade old, is still raw—and the ritual chorus of recriminations never changing. Like "the four questions" at a Passover seder, they're repeated each year when we gather together.

"You didn't foul that guy, Fred."

"No way."

"Bad call."

"Fuck that ref."

And we shake our heads once more at the injustice.

The next morning, after a tearful and heartfelt good-bye, Diana and I head out to California, in our "drive-away" car, a spacious, green Ford LTD. We have very little actual cash on hand, but we are loaded with barbeque meat. And we also have my father's Shell credit card, which is good for gas and food at Copper Penny restaurants. After all the time spent camping in our little tent and the hours of cramped hitching in the backs of trucks, this car feels like a hotel suite. Ubu can't believe he has the entire backseat to himself.

I'm driving this leg of the trip, the I-80 straight out west, with Diana alongside as navigator. She was a stewardess, and her father was a pilot, so she really knows how to read a map and is constantly adjusting our course looking for the most efficient route. No one in my family can *fold* a map, let alone read one.

"You can get off at the next exit and we can take the 510 over to the 20. It'll save about fifteen miles."

"I'm OK."

"You should get off."

I know I should, but I can't. With Jews and travel, once the course is set, it's very hard to deviate. This is difficult for Diana to understand, because on her family trips, the course was always plotted out in great detail. Various routes considered and rejected, others offered and accepted, and it was always a source of great pride to have arrived via the absolutely most efficient route possible.

In my family, we're glad if we arrive the same calendar year in which we leave. "We're here. We're alive. What's the difference how we came."

I want Diana to be happy, and so I get off at the 510 and head over to the 20. She's excited. This is the better way to go. I feel adventurous. I'm feeling like we're Lewis and Clark in an LTD, when I see the spinning red light and I hear the siren. It's a classic speed trap outside Clyde, Ohio, designed to catch guys whose wives or girlfriends have said, "Why don't we get off here, honey, and go over to the 510?" and the speed limit drops abruptly from sixty-five miles an hour to fifteen.

The cop is more or less what you'd expect plus ten pounds of hat. After a lecture on highway safety and some hemming and hawing, it becomes abundantly clear that what he's really looking for here is a bribe. "Hey, buddy, if only I could."

He ups the ante. With July Fourth weekend coming up, I'll have to stay in jail until Tuesday for my court date with the judge. Can't risk me fleeing the country. He's sorry there's nothing he can do. I'm sorry there's nothing I can do.

He takes the registration and my license, looks them over, and then looks back at me.

"Goldberg, huh?"

"Goldberg. Right."

I'm not expecting a Torah question.

"I was in the Marines with a Fred Goldberg. Great guy."

I look at him and say the first thing that comes into my mind.

"He's my brother."

I don't know where that came from, and I'm afraid that Diana might give birth right here in the front seat, but too late—it's out. Ubu peeks his head up in back. "Do I know Fred?"

"Love Fred," the fat cop says.

"Everybody does," I offer, hoping that it's true.

"How is old Freddie?"

"The same."

I don't know how much longer we can keep this up, and I'm hoping he can't hear my heart beating, because to me it sounds like a bass drum at a football game. I don't know what the penalty is for impersonating having a brother in the Marines, but I'm sure it's worse here in Clyde.

The fat cop's quiet for a beat. He can't give Fred's kid brother a ticket, can he? I point out that I, too, think it would be wrong, but I'm just one guy. Luckily, this cop is an idiot as well as a crook, and he lets us go scot-free.

As we drive away, I'm thinking to myself, how many Goldbergs are actually ever in the Marines at any one moment? And what are the odds of that guy being in the same unit with that cop? I begin to believe that maybe I do have a brother Fred. Or maybe just a guardian angel.

We get back on I-80 and head straight for Chicago now, eating as many meals as we can handle at the Copper Pennys along the way. My dad's letting us have that card is so typical of his generous nature. He has no clear understanding of what we're doing (as if we do), but he wants to be supportive of me and Diana any way he can. He's worked at two jobs for as long as I can remember. The main post office down near the Brooklyn Bridge by day. And the mail room at Merrill Lynch on Wall Street by night. When I left for school in the morning, he was asleep. And when I came home, he was at work. And yet, all through school, he never missed a game I played.

When I'd run out on the court, the first thing I'd do was try to find him in the stands. When I spotted him, he'd nod and give a smile and a wave. And that look that said, "I'm here for you." That said, "You're my boy and I love you, win or lose. And I always will, no matter what."

This theory was first tested when I lost my scholarship to Brandeis and dropped out. Tested a little bit more when I quit Hofstra two weeks before graduation and went off to be a waiter in Greenwich Village. Tested even further now, and perhaps to the limit, as Diana and I, unmarried, without visible means of support, and about to become parents, are motoring toward California on his dime.

But he will never waver. He will keep his end of the bargain. He never said he understood. But he always said, "I love you." As a parent myself now, I can only marvel at his tolerance and patience. At his absolute belief in me and what I would accomplish one day, when I "set my mind to it."

The reason we have to stop off in Chicago is to check in with the national headquarters of the drive-away company. They want to take a look at the car to make sure it's not been damaged. Also, it's a way to keep you on schedule, I guess. Anyway, it's all routine is what I'm thinking. Once again, I'm wrong.

The tiny office on Lakeshore Drive is jammed with young people looking to score cars to get out to California. We recognize a lot of the same faces from the Red Cross in Athens and the Travelers Aid in Paris.

We all smile, hug, do the peace sign, nod and mumble some "hey mans," and offer each other fruits and nuts.

Diana and I go in to see the manager. He checks our papers, checks the car, and everything seems to be OK. Then he asks to see $100 in cash. I explain to him that I don't have $100 in cash. That

I'll probably never have $100 in cash. But I do have this Shell credit card, which I display proudly while pointing out the additional benefits of being able to eat at Copper Penny restaurants across the land. He's not impressed, not even a little, and unless we can show him $100 in cash, he's going to take the car away and give it to one of the kids waiting in the outer office. I ask him for five minutes to just "think of something," and I step outside.

It's hot in Chicago. "Hog butcher to the world" hot, and I don't know what we're going to do. They're going to take the car. We'll be stranded in Chicago. I stand there for a minute, sweating, then I hear a voice, "Goldberg?"

I turn, and it's Paul Galka from the old neighborhood in Brooklyn. He sat in front of me in those classes where we were seated alphabetically. While one of the world's sweetest guys, Paul was never a serious scholar, and I happily carried him academically from seventh grade to high-school graduation. I haven't seen him in ten years.

"Goldberg, how are you?"

"Galka. I need a hundred dollars."

I explain to him what's going on, and he says not to worry. He owns the plant store next door, and he knows the drive-away manager really well. He goes inside and vouches for us. Then comes back out and gives us a hundred-dollar bill—takes us on a tour of Chicago, Wrigley Field, the art museum, gets us some insanely good Polish hot dogs, and then sends us on our way out west.

What a nice guy, Paul Galka. I can't help but think if he'd been more proficient in science and math, would he have been so nice? I think he would. But then again, what are the chances that Paul Galka from Brooklyn would own this plant store next to this drive-away office in Chicago and step outside at the exact moment that he did and rescue us? I look up to the heavens and thank Fred Goldberg one more time.

The rest of our trip out to California is thankfully uneventful, and we stop off now in Santa Cruz to visit Diana's family. This is the first time I'm going to be meeting her parents, Jack and Brenda Meehan. One day we will become incredibly close, and I will love them the way I love my own parents, and they will love me as their own son. Today is not that day.

Jack is an imposing man. An orphan, raised in the tough Red Hook section of Brooklyn with little or no formal education, he has worked his way up to the very highest levels of management at Lockheed Aerospace. At this moment, he is in charge of a team of engineers who are putting missiles up into space, and he looks like he'd be more than happy to find me a seat on any one of them.

A pilot in World War II, shot down twice, Jack's still active in the reserves, and politically he's a little to the right of John Wayne. Looking at Jack, you understand why we won World War II.

Brenda is a beautiful, gentle woman who immigrated to America from Ireland when she was twelve. A dancer, a poet. There's a light in her eyes that even this difficult situation cannot extinguish. But it is flickering a little weakly at the moment. She's a practicing Catholic, deeply spiritual, and her first instinct is to respond with tolerance and love, but this is not an easy time for her.

Looking at it from their point of view, it's not hard to understand their distress. Diana's pregnant. We're not married. We're not getting married. I'm not Catholic. I have long hair and a long beard. I have no job and I've made it pretty clear that I might never actually want one. Many years later, a father myself now, I said to Jack, "That boy walks into my house today, with my daughter, I shoot him."

Jack looked at me and smiled.

"I thought about it."

That night in '72, even though we've lived together three years and Diana is pregnant, Jack and Brenda would prefer for us to sleep in separate rooms. I'm all right with it. I feel I'm causing these people enough pain already. I don't need to add to it. This turns out to be a big problem for Ubu, though. It's always been the three of us sleeping together, and he doesn't know where to go now. He starts out with Diana, in her old room. Then, when he gets nervous about me, he scratches on the door to Diana's brother Tom's room, where I am. Then back to Diana. Then back to me. I'm getting worried. Ubu likes to get his eight hours, and the last thing we need right now is to be traveling tomorrow with a sleep-deprived Labrador.

The next morning, we gather to say good-bye, and everyone's still a little tense. Apparently, Ubu wasn't the only one who didn't sleep. I feel bad for Jack and Brenda, but I don't know what to do or what to say. They're worried about their daughter, whom they love deeply. To Brenda, marriage is a sacrament, and she can't understand why her daughter is against it. The fact that we're not married poses a similar problem for my family. But they deal with it in the same manner they deal with all their problems. They just pretend we're married. They always ask politely, "How's your wife?" and that seems to work for them.

Back in Berkeley now, we're searching for a way that we can make a living yet still be together all the time. I can't imagine going off to work and leaving Ubu behind, let alone Diana and our baby. We come up with an idea. What if we opened up a day-care center? We could rent a big old Victorian. Use the upstairs for ourselves, and have the downstairs for the center. Our baby would have a built-in "family" of friends, be with both her parents all the time, and maybe we'll even make a little money if we have to.

We need a name, and Diana comes up with the "Organic Day Care Center." We are in Berkeley, after all, and it's always good to know your audience. Now we need a slogan. I offer, "Rain or Shine We Take Your Kid on a Trip Every Day." Again, know your audience.

We put posters up in every bookstore, co-op, health-food store, and music store we can find. We get some second-hand toys from the flea markets around town. Get donations of paints and supplies from artist friends. Sign up other friends to do music and mime, to do yoga (it would be an elective), and immerse ourselves in early-childhood education literature. *The Magic Years,* by Selma H. Fraiberg, becomes our bible.

Diana has a teaching credential, and even though it's for high-school English, it does lend an air of respectability to the venture. The fact that I'm a father-to-be, an actual guy, is also a big selling point. Most of our kids will be from single-parent families, mostly single moms, and they like the idea of there being a man in the house.

Ubu is also a reassuring fixture to prospective parents. And look-ing at him, I have to admit he does possess a certain calm, avuncu-lar presence, reminding me at times of Fred MacMurray in *My Three Sons.* Later, playing in the park with our kids, Ubu would circle endlessly around them, protectively patrolling the perimeter, keeping a wary eye out for child molesters and cats.

Housed in a beautiful old building on the Oakland–Berkeley border, the Organic Day Care Center is an instant success. We're charging one hundred dollars a month, and we have to cap the number of children we can take at twelve. This seems to be the maximum number we can handle and still provide a quality envi-ronment and answer all the penis and vagina questions that come our way.

True to our mission, we use only organic foods, and we do take the group out on a trip every day to a park or a museum or up to the lake. Diana and I scrupulously take turns sharing all the different roles equally. Driving, cooking, arts and crafts, sports. We want the kids to notice how none of these tasks is gender specific. We're relentless about this, to the point that one day little Jenny Ganz tells me, "I know girls can do anything. But we like it better when Diana makes lunch."

I do love watching Diana with the kids. She's so patient. A natu-ral teacher. Never passes up a chance to offer encouragement and sup-port. Ubu's also displaying a patience that I didn't know he had. He will allow kids to jump on him, squeeze him, pet him. He does, however, draw the line at trying to grab his balls. But even then he'll just turn away and mumble one quick bark. Never a growl. I'd like to see Fred MacMurray display that kind of grace in a similar situation.

Meanwhile, we're all waiting anxiously for the new baby, whom we're expecting to arrive sometime in December. But on October 29, she decides it's time to make her appearance.

{ c h a p t e r   n i n e }

*I*t has been a beautiful fall Saturday in the Bay Area, and we've taken full advantage, spending most of the afternoon across the bridge, in San Francisco. We play with Ubu in Golden Gate Park, walk through the Presidio, snack along Fisherman's Wharf. We have just returned home, and I am setting the table for dinner, when Diana steps out of the kitchen and stands there in the doorway.

"My water broke."

Since I thought this event was at least two months away, it didn't register at first, and I thought she was talking about the Sparkletts bottle in the corner, and I'm wondering why she's suddenly so possessive about that. "*My* water?"

"I didn't hear anything."

I look over her shoulder and see the jug still intact there on its perch.

"My water broke. The baby's coming."

"Are you sure?" I ask helpfully. "I mean, I'm not a doctor. But this is supposed to happen in December, isn't it?"

She has the good sense to ignore me and go upstairs to pack for the trip to the hospital. I set and unset the table a few dozen times and then stretch out in front of the fireplace for a minute to think about the magnitude of the upcoming birth, and what it means.

84

When Diana wakes me, it's morning.

"It's time to go."

You have to love the Irish in these situations. She has called the hospital, organized everything, and packed the car, while she let me sleep the whole night in front of the fire.

"Are you OK to drive?" she asks, "I know you're rested."

Because we believed we had at least two months before the actual birth date, we had not yet enrolled in any natural childbirth classes. The good news is, we have the book *Thank You, Dr. Lamaze*, by Marjorie Karmel. The bad news is, we haven't read it. I'm used to pulling all-nighters before an exam, but this is pushing the envelope.

In the waiting room I'm reading to Diana from the Lamaze book, while at the same time, in the margins, I'm noting times of the contractions. Evidently, I'm not reading fast enough.

"'You will experience a slight pressure on the . . .'"

"I'm past that! I'm past that!"

I flip a few more pages.

"'At this point the breathing will become . . .'"

"I'm past that, I tell you! Get to where the baby's coming."

I look over and, in Diana's eyes, I see a look that's similar to a look I'd seen on a mother tiger, in an episode of *Wild Kingdom* where Marlon Perkins almost got his head ripped off. The nurse comes in and takes the book out of my hands.

"Little late for that, isn't it, kids?" She laughs as she wheels us off to the delivery room. Diana makes me promise that I won't let them give her any drugs. I promise.

"I'm serious."

"I know."

"Look at me."

She has the "tiger-mother" look again, and I think I hear some growling.

"No drugs. Got it."

We are enrolled in the public health-assistance program at this point, and we almost never see the same doctor twice. The doctor on call today, Dr. Dempsey, is also new to us. A handsome young African-American man, he gives us a reassuring smile as we come in.

As they're preparing Diana and making her comfortable, I notice Dr. Dempsey's stealing looks at me like he's seen me somewhere before. I'm hoping it's not *Under the Yum Yum Tree.* Some people hold a grudge.

"Didn't you play basketball for Lafayette?"

"Yeah. I was captain of the team in '62."

This being no time, I feel, to hide my light under a bushel.

"Goldberg, right? Gary?"

"Yeah."

"Rick Dempsey, I played against you in the Kelly Park tournament."

Dempsey was a year or two ahead of me. Went to Erasmus. We cannot believe how excited we are to see each other again. We quickly run through the names of the more than five hundred people we know in common, and then we hear Diana, loud: "Guys! Having a baby here!" I step back to let Dr. Dempsey do his work. But I'm feeling confident now, because, as I recall, Dempsey did have very quick hands, and a soft touch.

The birth goes very smoothly, and I remember it as not being very painful for me at all. Along with the talented nurses who helped me "coach," and the talented Dr. Dempsey at the helm, and the talented and brave Diana, we've delivered a beautiful, healthy baby girl, six pounds, nine ounces, Shana Colleen. One name for each side of the family.

Diana and I now throw ourselves into parenting as if we are the first two people ever to do this. Every piece of food that Shana gets is either grown by friends or grown by us. Everything 100 percent organic. Vegetables pureed at home. Milk from cows serenaded by Irish tenors, high up in the mountains of Tibet. My closest friend is now the Dy-Dee Diaper guy, who seems to live with us.

"Did you play basketball with him too?" Diana wants to know.

She's still not completely over the male bonding thing she witnessed between me and Dr. Dempsey.

We have 104 baby monitors spread throughout the house, and at the first hint of a cry from Shana, we race upstairs to rescue her. Marcia, a nurse friend of ours, is afraid that if we keep that up Shana's lungs will never get a chance to fully develop. "It's OK to let her cry a little," she tells us. That can't be right.

Shana is an easy baby. And an easy baby to love. Not only does she very quickly begin to sleep through the night, but even when she wakes up in the morning, rather than calling out for help, she stays in her crib and plays with her mobiles, singing and chirping. When we do go in to get her, she squeals with delight when we reach in to pick her up. She's healthy. She's happy. In every picture we have of her as a baby, she's smiling widely.

The kids at the center are also incredibly excited about *their* baby Shana. She's like a new doll for them. They take turns holding her, giving her a bottle, singing to her. Every time she comes down in the morning, they wait at the bottom of the stairs and call her name and cheer. Shana gets used to people breaking into applause when she enters a room. She smiles and takes it in, "Yes, I'm here, and you may adore me." Behavior I would come to recognize later in certain television stars I'd get to work with.

Diana's parents have still not seen the baby, but they're on their way up this afternoon. It was Brenda's idea, and initially Jack resisted.

Then Brenda said, "Look, this is my daughter, and this is her baby, and I'm going up to see them. If you don't want to go, I'll go myself."

Jack said, "If you're going to go, I may as well drive you," and that explains the green Oldsmobile Toronado hovering in our driveway.

Brenda is immediately and completely in love with the baby. She holds Shana, who smiles up at her. "She looks like your Aunt Maureen," Brenda coos. I think she looks like my cousin Miriam, but I don't want to start any trouble. Jack is more wary. He just can't get his head around this.

It's time for Shana's lunch, and Diana hands her off to me, to take her into the kitchen and feed her. Brenda says to Jack, "Why don't you go with him and help?"

Jack looks over at me.

"I could use some help."

We move into the kitchen, and I ask Jack to hold Shana while I prepare the bottle for her. He's bouncing Shana up and down now, talking baby talk. She's gurgling back sounds of love. I come over and take Shana out of Jack's hands. "Easy," he cautions me. I put her in my lap, tilt her head back, and begin to give her the bottle. "Careful. You don't want to tilt her head back that much," he tells me. I offer him the bottle to feed her himself. He takes it and begins to feed. It's been a while, but it all comes back to him, and there's gentleness and love in every drop he delivers. We take turns feeding and burping. I tell him about the day-care center. How great it is to be together with Shana and Diana all day. What we're learning from the kids. He talks about being overseas when Diana was born. How difficult it was to be separated. How in those days fathers weren't really so hands-on. I ask him if he wants to change the diaper. That's more hands-on than he had in mind.

We finish feeding Shana, I finish changing the diaper, and we're about to head back out and find the "girls." Jack stops me; there are tears in his eyes.

"Look, I don't understand what's going on here, and it's really hard for me to accept it. But there's so much love in this house between you and my daughter and this baby. You have to show me how to be a part of it."

I hug Jack, maybe the first man ever to do so, and slowly, tentatively, he hugs me back. We're both teary-eyed now. And I have more respect for this man than any man I've ever known.

1984

{ chapter ten }

We've finished our second year on NBC. The show, which started out slowly, has been steadily building. We are usually number two in our time slot, behind *Magnum, P.I.,* a runaway hit on CBS starring Tom Selleck.

I can tell the ratings race has tightened, because Selleck seems to be doing a lot more scenes without his shirt on. I like *Magnum.* It has Selleck's easygoing charm, great scenery, and snappy dialogue. I can understand why people would want to watch it. I just wish they'd stop.

Brandon Tartikoff points out two developments trending in our favor. One: We're occasionally beating *Magnum* in the overnights, the breakdown of the major big-city markets. When the rest of the country reports in, a day or two later, *Magnum's* back to number one. But Brandon says that's the way it happens. First you win the major markets, then the rest of the country will follow. Two: We're heading into reruns now, and the one-hour shows, even ones as popular as *Magnum,* don't seem to fare as well in reruns. Brandon predicts we will begin to overtake *Magnum* by the summer's end.

Brandon's prediction does, in fact, come to pass. In reruns that spring and summer, we begin to tighten the ratings gap. One week, in the New York City area, we're even the number-one show, of all shows. And when my sister-in-law, Lena, comes back one day from a health-care conference, where one of the panelists accused another panelist of trying to "Alex Keaton" him, I take it as a good sign. Alex is becoming a verb.

Between Diana teaching at UCLA, me doing the show, the usual car-pooling and soccer schedule, and with a second daughter, Cailin, now a year old, life is pretty hectic. We rarely socialize, but one night we do, surprisingly, find ourselves in Bel-Air, at a real Hollywood extravaganza at the home of a well-known and, judging from the twenty-five-minute drive from the front gate to the main house, very wealthy studio chief. It's the kind of place where you go, "Oh, look! That's a great copy of Monet's Water Lilies," and then you realize that it's not a copy.

At dinner, I'm seated next to the studio chief, and he likes *Family Ties,* he tells me, and if I'm ever interested in moving over to the film world, he has some projects I might find interesting. He takes my plastic name tag off my jacket (yes, everyone had a name tag), and dramatically slaps the tag on his forehead to remind himself that he's to call me first thing in the morning.

It's hard to talk to a guy who's wearing your name tag on his head, but I do my best. I explain that I'm busy with the show. And when I'm not working on *Family Ties,* I don't like to do other projects, because it takes away from my time with my family.

"It's difficult to have a career and a real family life in Hollywood," he tells me. "Eventually, you'll give up one of them, you'll see. You'll give up your family. Most people do."

I say, "Excuse me." I take Diana's hand and we get up, and we immediately leave the party and go home. That guy never called me either.

As we get ready, now, for the third season, Brandon has news about the fall schedule. They're going to move us to Thursday night at 8:30, behind a new show they've picked up after ABC turned it down, *The Cosby Show.* I am not happy.

"Jeez, Brandon, this guy's failed in three different TV series. He's doing Jell-O commercials."

"Just look at the pilot."

"We're just beginning to hit our stride. You said so yourself."

"Just look at the pilot."

"We're winning some of the big-city markets. We're on the verge of becoming a hit show, and now we're going to get dragged down by Bill Cosby."

"Just look at the pilot."

I look at the pilot. Written by Ed. Weinberger, directed by Jay Sandrich, of *Mary Tyler Moore* fame, based primarily on Cosby's nightclub act. It is one of the funniest and most appealing TV shows I've ever seen. Cosby is brilliant. The kids are great, and Phylicia Rashad is perfect as Cosby's wife. I call up Brandon and thank him. And begin to look for beachfront property in Hawaii.

Thursday night on NBC quickly becomes "must see" TV. *Cosby's* the number-one show every week. We're the number-two show, with *Cheers, Night Court,* and *Hill Street Blues* all in the top ten. One Friday morning, driving over to Paramount, I notice a long line of people camped out on Gower Street. There are beach chairs, blankets, some sleeping bags. When I ask the guard about it, he tells me, "They're waiting to see your show."

I walk over to talk to the people in line. Some did, actually, sleep over the night before. They talk about what the show means to them. How much they love this Keaton family. How much they love Alex.

"He's like my brother."

"He's like my son."

"They call me Alex at school."

When I first created the character of Alex Keaton, I considered many of his character traits a liability. His conservative politics. His obsession with money and success. Which seemed more suited, in my mind, to a man in his early fifties than to a boy of seventeen. But right from the beginning, all the mail we received, especially from kids Alex's age, was about how much they respected him, and how much they wanted to be like him.

A lot of the credit (or blame) for this has to go to Michael Fox himself. Audiences were so captivated by him, and so charmed by him, that it was easy for them to want to "be like Mike" and want to be on his side. Whatever harsh theories or concepts Alex put forth, the audience simply refused to acknowledge the dark side of whatever he was saying.

The final *New York Times* review, in reference to Alex Keaton, coined a phrase which sums it up for me, "Greed, with the face of an angel."

As the mail comes pouring in now, much of it in pencil and crayon, I'm struck by how isolated some of our younger viewers seem to be. From their community, and, in many cases, from their own families. It's clear that the Keatons are not a "fictional" family to them, but rather people they feel close to. Closer, in fact, than anyone else they know.

"Could you call my father? He doesn't talk to me the way Mr. Keaton talks to Alex."

"That happened to me. What happened to Mallory. But I couldn't tell nobody."

I'm a little overwhelmed by this position of responsibility we seem to have inherited. I'm nervous we could do some inadvertent harm here. We're just trying to make people laugh.

I reach out to the academic community, talk to teachers in the field, guidance counselors, child psychologists. Start going to seminars and retreats on family issues.

In return we begin, now, to get requests from these same teachers, doctors, counselors, asking for copies of specific episodes of our show, so they can use them as teaching tools. They explain that their patients or students can speak more openly about whatever issues are involved in their own lives, when they can talk about it as if it was something that was Mallory's problem. Or Alex's.

I originally thought *Family Ties* would be a show centered on the parents, who were, after all, based on me and Diana. And I thought we would explore the big themes—nuclear war, racism, censorship, corruption in politics, etc. While we do, at one time or another, deal with all these issues (with varying degrees of success), the heart of the show, due in no small part to Mike's extraordinary appeal and the appeal of Justine Bateman, who's becoming a star in her own right, becomes the kids. And our best episodes are always about those small, recognizable intrafamily moments. The angst of growing up. Alex has two dates for the prom. Mallory can't get into the sorority she wants to join. Jennifer doesn't want to be on a softball team where her father is the coach.

We find our best story ideas seem to come from our own lives or lives of friends. In my own family, Diana and Shana, who's a teenager now, are slowly catching on to the idea that anything they do, can and will be used against them on network television. One time, after an argument, Diana tells me, "And I don't want to see this next week on *Family Ties.*"

Shana, who is as smart as Alex but can shop with Mallory, accuses me of always rewriting my own behavior and making the father on the show look good. "It's my show," I tell her. "You want to look better, get your own show."

And one day, she will. Right out of college, writing with her then boyfriend, now husband, Scott Silveri, and using assumed names, at first, so I can't help them, they get signed by ICM. They go out on three interviews. I caution them that it's going to take time. Rejection is part of this business, you can't take it personally. They get offered all three jobs. Sign with *Mad About You,* where they work for one season as staff writers, and are then hired away by *Friends,* where they will stay eight years and eventually rise to executive producers and head writers, and win Emmys of their own. And if you're ever watching episodes of *Friends* in reruns, and you notice some erratic behavior from Monica's parents, especially the father, played by Elliot Gould, that very well could be me.

We've added a couple of new writers to our team. Alan Uger, a former dentist, who'd been a writer on the Mel Brooks movie *Blazing Saddles.* Alan was also a charter member of the New York City

Stickball Team, an improv group featuring a young comic genius, Robert Klein. Alan will add a strong, funny voice for Steven Keaton.

And then one day I come into my office and pull a spec *Family Ties* script from a huge pile of specs on my desk. It's written by a Marc Lawrence, out in Long Island, and it's come in unsolicited. I start to read it and it's immediately clear that it's good. It's very good. In fact, it's as good as anything we're doing.

I call Marc Lawrence up. Tell him how much I like the script. He tells me a little bit about his "story." On the advice of his Constitutional Law Professor, John Sexton,* Marc has dropped out of NYU Law School to try comedy writing, and this is his first script attempt. I offer him a job on the show. I'd like him to come out as soon as he can.

"California?" he whines. "I don't know."

"Where did you think we did the show?"

"I know, I know. But, I don't like to fly. And, I have to pack. . . ."

"No, you know what? You're right. You stay there. We'll move the show to Long Island."

Marc comes out—by airplane, I'm happy to report. He's an interesting cross between Hugh Grant and Woody Allen. He's in a Beatles T-shirt and shorts, has on red high-top tennis shoes.

"My mother told me to wear a suit, but I don't have one."

I put my arms out.

"Come. You've come to the right place. Welcome."

Marc will go on to a big career as a feature film writer-director, creating such blockbuster hits as *Miss Congeniality* and *Two Weeks Notice.* With Marc and Michael Weithorn, I'm now working with two brilliant young writers, and two really sweet guys.

Years later Marc and Michael would confess that on slow days, just to see me come unglued, they would intentionally pitch the worst possible *Family Ties* idea to me, just to see me explode.

---

*John Sexton would later become the president of NYU. But I believe his real purpose here on earth was to talk Marc Lawrence out of becoming a lawyer. And for that, his place in heaven is secure.

"Boss, hear us out." They liked to call me "boss" like in the old '40s gangster movies.

"Boss, listen to the whole pitch before you say anything, OK?"

"OK."

"This may not seem like an obvious episode, but we like it. We know it could be controversial."

"What's the idea?"

Long silence, then: "Steven and Elyse decide to have an open marriage."

"What?"

"This could be very helpful to the swinger community."

"What swinger community?"

"They're out there, boss. And they watch a lot of TV."

"How do they find time?"

And then I would start raving madly, and they would shake their heads, "Sorry, boss, sorry," and leave.

They said in all the time they pitched the crazy ideas trying to get me to explode, I never once let them down.

We all live for Friday night, the tape night for *Family Ties,* which has become a rock-and-roll show. The long lines on Gower Street keep getting longer and, once inside stage 24 and in their seats, the fans are noisy and excited. They lean forward all the time now. For everyone.

Mike Fox and I approach each show night as if we're getting ready for a "big game." Like two lunatic jocks playing for the state championship. Between scenes I run back with him to his dressing room. It's our last chance to go over any late changes in that scene. Ask and answer questions of each other. Mike's eyes are wide now and he looks to me like a linebacker getting ready. My eyes must be wide, too, because Mike looks a little scared. We're doing everything but banging our heads together.

What's great about the high-wire act of half-hour TV comedy is you can't fake it. Either the audience laughs or they don't. If they laugh, you win. If they don't, you lose. Most of the time we win. BIG.

After the show, we're still too high to come back down, and most Friday nights we'll go out for late dinner and a drink. The writers, our director, a couple of the actors, usually Mike and Justine, some of the crew people, and everybody's families. We usually go over to St. Germain, an elegant French place on Melrose, near the Studio. They know we come in every Friday night, and they have our corner saved. The staff, led by headwaiter Rayjean Fontaine, is like family by now, and we all hug and kiss on the way in and out. Mike usually picks up the bar tab for everyone. I pick up the food.

The theme for the evening is "excess," as we try, two working-class kids like Michael and me, to make some sense of the level of success we're flirting with here. Somehow the world has cracked open just a little at the top and allowed the two of us to squeeze through. And it seems the only way to make it all acceptable, somehow, is to make fun of it. To go to St. Germain, the priciest, fanciest place in town, and make it our clubhouse. To order one of every main dish on the menu and two of all the desserts.

One night, after a particularly good show, and after a couple of particularly good bottles of particularly good Tattinger red champagne, Mike and I find ourselves seated, just the two of us, in one of the back corner booths at St. Germain. We're still flushed from tonight's success. Mike looks out across the restaurant, crowded now with our family and friends. He smiles, looks over at me, and gives a little laugh.

"It's like we jumped a life, you know?"

1974

{ c h a p t e r   e l e v e n }

Whatever we pay preschool teachers in this country, it's not enough. The job is monumental and all-consuming. Even at night, Diana and I find all we can talk about is what happened that day with the kids. It becomes impossible to hang out with anyone except other day-care providers. Our knowledge of popular songs is reduced to "I'm a Little Teapot," "If You're Happy and You Know It," "Wheels on the Bus"—the classics. And one night at dinner, when I ask Diana to pass me a glass of "wa-wa," we realize that we may have crossed the line. It's been great for us, great for Shana. But after two years, we're exhausted, and it's time to move on.

After one final blowout party, featuring bottomless cups of apple juice and every mime-friend we can round up, we turn the center over to a young couple, Seth and Carol, who have a new baby of their own and will carry on in our tradition. We will be moving down to San Diego, where Diana will pursue a master's degree in communication at San Diego State. I will tag along, taking care of Shana, looking out for Ubu. At the very last moment, I decide I may as well enroll there myself, in what will now become the thirteenth year of my quest for that elusive bachelor of arts degree.

Diana is happy to be back in an academic environment, and she's taking full advantage. She's pursuing a double master's degree in mass communication and women's studies while also teaching three undergraduate courses and taking graduate classes in English and art history. I'm trying to avoid having to take math I for the eleventh time.

We rent a cheap little Spanish bungalow not far from campus. With Diana's $350 per month, food stamps, and some student loans, we're managing to get by. We can't afford any of the luxuries, like furniture, or a phone. But it appears I'll be able to hold on to all my blood for a while, and that's comforting.

In an effort to painlessly fulfill some general education requirements, I sign up for a writing class in the Telecommunication and Film Department. The teacher is Nate Monaster, a professional writer down in San Diego for this one semester as their Visiting Artist in Residence. It doesn't sound too difficult. It might be fun. If nothing else, it'll bring me three units closer to that B.A.*

Nate Monaster began his career in radio in the 1950s, as a writer on *Duffy's Tavern.* He has an Academy Award nomination for *That Touch of Mink,* with Cary Grant, and he's a former president of the Writer's Guild of America. He's also a compassionate, generous, and thoughtful man, and he will change my life forever. Not very often can you point to that one person and say, "Yeah, him. I owe it all to him." Well, I can point and say, "I owe it all to Nate Monaster."

The assignment for the class that week was to write a television commercial, a project for which I really didn't have much interest. I asked Nate if I could write something else. Maybe something more personal. He encouraged that idea and I went off to see if I could, in fact, write "something else."

I thought I'd try to write about the time I spent working as a waiter at the Village Gate in the mid 1960s. It was an exhilarating time for me. My introduction to Greenwich Village, to the world of artists and musicians, and dreamers. My first tentative steps toward redefining myself, moving out of the sports culture, which had dominated and defined my life, and toward a more gentle version of myself.

---

*Also in this class is future Academy Award–winning producer, Kathy Kennedy.

When I sat down to write, I was amazed to discover that I could easily place myself back in that dark, cavernous room on Bleecker Street. I could hear the music again. The laughter of the quintessential New York crowd. I could remember entire conversations. What people were wearing. What they looked like. Before I knew it, I had written twenty-five or thirty pages, which I nervously handed in to Nate Monaster's class the next morning.

Two days later my neighbor, Dan, came over and said I had a phone call. Someone from the college. We had used Dan's phone as our contact number at the school, and I hurried across the yard to his house to take the call.

"Hello."

"Is this Gary Goldberg?"

"Yeah."

"This is Nate Monaster. Can you come in and see me?"

"OK. When should I—"

"Why don't you come now?"

I walked dejectedly back across the yard to our bungalow, where Diana was waiting.

"What's the matter?"

"My writing class. The teacher wants to see me. This can't be good."

"You don't know that."

"C'mon, I obviously did something wrong, or I wouldn't have to go in and see him *right now.* I can't believe I'm screwing up college again."

At the El Nido apartments, which have been converted into the TV-Film offices, I climb the steps to the second floor and knock on Nate Monaster's office door, and enter. He's seated at his desk, and I can see my work spread out in front of him.

"I'm Gary Goldberg. You wanted to see me."

Nate looks up kindly. "You're Gary Goldberg?"

"Yeah."

He stares at me for a long moment. "You're a writer, Gary."

"Huh?"

"You're a writer. I don't want you in this class. I have nothing to teach you. You have a unique style, and I don't want to get in the way."

I'm not sure I'm hearing this correctly. Or how excited I should get. I mean, I'm thirty years old. I have a family. I'm not going to get too excited because I'm going to get an A in the class. Although it would be my first.

"I'm not sure I understand what you're saying, exactly."

"I'm saying you're a writer. What are your favorite television shows?"

I explain that we don't have a television set. That we haven't watched TV in years. Nate says maybe we should get one, and maybe I should "take a look." He thinks it's something I could do. He promises to get me copies of scripts of any shows I do like, so I can see the proper form and format. Get a sense of how they do it. In the meantime, he's going to call some agents he knows, to see if anyone might be interested in representing me.

I try to thank him as profusely as I can, while still retaining some shred of dignity and decorum. I come close, but in the end I fail, and he has to peel me off him.

Diana's excited about the news and wants to go out and celebrate. I point out that no money actually changed hands, but she's adamant. This is a special day. I've been recognized. I'm going to be a writer.

We go off to McDonald's, which is at the upper limits of our budget, but this will be a night to throw caution to the wind. Whatever you say about McDonald's and the way their food can make you incredibly fat, raise your blood pressure, and then kill you, I will always keep a soft spot in my heart for the Golden Arches. When it was a very big deal to be able to go out to eat, they provided us with an affordable "night on the town." The staff was always courteous and cheerful, and once you cleared away your trays and laid out your burgers and fries and tucked in your napkins, it could feel like the A table at Spago, and it certainly did to us that night.

Diana raised her Styrofoam cup of tea. I raised mine to her.

"You're a writer."

"We don't know that for sure."

"Yes we do." She clinked my cup and smiled. "Yes we do."

The next morning, we hear about a motel in Pacific Beach that's going out of business, selling off all their furniture and appliances. It might be a good place for us to go to get a cheap TV. A friend of ours, Rusty Cramer, has a pickup truck, and he agrees to take us out there. When we walk into the motel, right there in the lobby is a big black-and-white TV set, which they're selling for twenty-five dollars. It's a tax deduction, I'm thinking, not that I've ever made enough money to pay taxes.

Back at the house, we plug in the big, bulky set and turn it on. There's a cop show playing, *Get Christie Love!*, starring Teresa Graves. I stand there and watch for about five minutes, and then I turn to Diana.

"I can do that. I can definitely do that."

I start to watch TV every night now, to see which shows I might like. I'm really lucky, because there are so many fine comedies on at this particular time. *Mary Tyler Moore, Bob Newhart, M*A*S*H, All in the Family, Barney Miller*, just to name a few. Nate Monaster gets me the scripts for these shows, and I start studying them. On the one hand, it's a little scary. These scripts are so good. So smart. So funny. On the other hand, it's exciting to see if I can measure up.

I love writing. Maybe I'm just shallow, but I don't find it hard or painful or lonely, and I'm turning out a new spec script every three days, it seems. Nate Monaster patiently reads my scripts, gives thoughtful criticism, and sends me back to do another draft or two or six. It doesn't matter. For the first time in my life I've found something to equal the passion and dedication I had for sports. I write eighteen hours a day. I don't get tired. All the old clichés come back. "When the going gets tough, the tough get going."

"It's not the size of the man in the fight, but the size of the fight in the man." I'm not sure if I'm writing or I'm playing basketball, but I can sense there's a similar relationship between hard work and success.

True to his word, Nate Monaster has sent a couple of my scripts up to Los Angeles, and there's some interest from a young agent who's just starting out, Jim Preminger. Jim's opening the literary department for the firm Bresler, Wolf, Cota and Livingston, who have among their clients a young actor they're very high on by the name of Jack Nicholson. Anyway, Jim Preminger would like to meet me. And one day later that week, I set out to hitchhike up to Beverly Hills to meet with him.

Thumb out, standing on the side of the I-5 heading north, I have no way of knowing that I will like Jim Preminger and he will like me. That he will be my agent for more than twenty years and will always offer thoughtful advice and counsel. Always put my interests before his. That we will win Emmys and become wealthy. At this moment, I'm not thinking about any of that. I'm just hopin' for a ride in a comfortable car.

Jim is not a typical agent. For one thing, he's tall, six four. The average height for an agent being four eleven. For another thing, he's an intellectual. He was a political science major at the University of Chicago. He's also very soft-spoken. Several times I have to ask him to speak up. When he does pump up the volume a bit, I get that what he's saying is he likes the scripts of mine he's read and he would like to represent me. We shake hands. I have an agent.

Back in San Diego, I'm turning out spec scripts at an alarming rate and sending them up to Jim Preminger. I've even started branching out and writing original specs, which I'm also sending up. Jim's been circulating these scripts to producers and story editors around town. People seem interested. Very complimentary about the writing. Really looking forward to reading the next script I write. It's actually a firm no, but we're both too naïve to realize it.

Diana's closing in on her master's degree, which she will receive next term. She has, of course, received all A's, has become the star of the department, and is being courted by several Ph.D. programs, including the Doctoral Communication Program at USC. I am also scheduled to receive my B.A. and graduate next term. However, at the last minute, after one and a half years at San Diego, two years at Brandeis, three years at Hofstra, semesters scattered about at Long Beach State, UC Berkeley, and San Francisco State, after thirteen years in college, I am told I'm still short one unit of biology.

I go to the head of the Biology Department, Dr. Claude Merzbacher, and explain my story. I've been in college since the presidency of John F. Kennedy. I have a family. Diana's going to be teaching at USC. I'm going up to L.A. with her to try to be a comedy writer. I love biology as much as the next guy, but I don't have time to make up this one unit.

Dr. Merzbacher's great. He totally gets it, and tells me he'll give me the one unit. Three conditions. One: Go out in the backyard tonight and write a page or two about what I see and hear. Two: I have to promise that if I ever write about scientists in general, and biologists in particular, I will portray them in a positive light. And three: If I ever win an award or I'm asked to make a speech, I will give the audience one scientific fact to take home with them. I promise. I get my one unit, and I graduate.

Three years later I will win the Writers Guild Award for Best Comedy Script for an episode of *M*A*S*H*. Nate Monaster will be in the audience. I have the privilege of thanking him publicly for all he's done for me. And then I tell those assembled: "Photosynthesis is a process by which energy in sunlight is used to convert water and carbon dioxide into carbohydrates and oxygen."

{chapter twelve}

*A*s a pre-graduation present, Grandma has sent us plane tickets to come visit them in Florida. After Grandpa died and my dad retired from the post office, my parents and my grandmother moved down there to Century Village, in West Palm Beach, where the three of them share a two-bedroom apartment. All my relatives on my grandmother's side and half their friends from the old neighborhood have also moved down to Florida. It's Bensonhurst South. I have been down to visit them once before, with Shana, when she was nine months old. But this will be the first time they get to meet Diana. Ubu has declined to accompany us to witness this historic first meeting, but he wants a full report when we get back.

As we're banking into the airport at West Palm Beach, as she's mere moments away from meeting my family for the first time, I look over at my beautiful life partner. Daughter of a rocket scientist, grew up in New Mexico, Colorado, California, convent-trained, about to receive her master's degree, going on to get her Ph.D. I put my hand on her knee.

"Nothing in your life has prepared you for what you are about to see."

Century Village is a walled and gated community with a very diverse population—50 percent Eastern European Jews and 50 percent Jews from other places. It's basically a little shtetl, and the walls are already up, so in case there's going to be another pogrom, no one will have to bother building them. In many ways, it's like visiting sixteenth-century Romania. Except there are golf carts.

My father's dressed in bright, greenish plaid pants. He has on a canary-yellow polo shirt to go with that. And he's wearing white vinyl shoes and a white plastic belt. He looks like he lost a bet.

"This is what they wear down here," he tells me.

I point out I don't think he looks that comfortable.

He shrugs, "What's the difference?" This is what they wear, so this is what he'll wear. It's easier that way.

That's my father in his main role: making it easier for everybody else. Just trying to keep the peace and please everyone. Years later, when he was diagnosed with lung cancer, the doctors told him he had two more years to live. And so he lived two more years, almost exactly. I always thought if they had told him he had five more years to live, he would have lived five more years. Whatever they wanted. Whatever made them happy.

At his funeral, my brother and I tried to think of a time when Dad had ever been mad at us. When he had ever yelled. When he had ever even raised his voice. We couldn't think of one.

Diana and I go to sleep that first night, in Florida, on the pull-out couch in the living room, with Shana between us.

"Do they always all talk at the same time?" Diana wants to know.

"Oh yeah."

"And did you notice if you ask your father a question your grandmother answers?"

"Oh yeah."

"And if you ask your mother a question your grandmother answers?"

"Oh yeah."

As I start to shrug myself awake the next morning, I have the odd feeling there are other people there in the room with me. I may still be dreaming, but it seems like I can hear some mumbling in a foreign language, some scraping of chairs, and as I start to sit up, the mumbling gets louder and I hear, "He's up, he's up," and the footsteps of people scrambling back into the room.

As my eyes clear, I see I wasn't dreaming. Because seated at the foot of the bed, on folding chairs, are all my relatives. They whisper good-mornings, and as Diana starts to rise, they actually gasp and ooh and ahh. She gives me a scared look. "Who are these people?"

They all begin to speak at once, several speaking in Yiddish, and they're speaking about us, as if we're not in the room.

My aunt Rose—famous in the family for the time she was watching *Bowling for Dollars* and casually offered up, "God, I hope the colored couple doesn't win"—is studying Diana intently. "Beautiful skin, Ruby, did you ever see skin like this? I'm asking you."

"Lovely skin," Uncle Ruby agrees.

"But, she has no nose. Ruby, look, that's not a nose."

Shana starts crying, and that sends everyone scurrying out of the room amid recriminations about whose fault it was, and my father comes over and restores some sense of sanity, and at least he apologizes. He didn't think they should be here when we woke up. "But everyone's so excited that you're here, and you know your grandma."

"Oh yeah."

The visit actually goes surprisingly well. My folks have clearly gone to a lot of trouble to make this a fun time for us and to welcome Diana into the family. There are a few holdouts. Aunt Rose for one. There's just never going to be enough nose there for her, but we're willing to let Aunt Rose go.

When my folks introduce Diana to the neighbors, she's always introduced the same way.

"She's not Jewish, but she's been to Israel."

This is always met with nods of approval. Some questions about the Holy Land then follow, and the encounter usually ends with some story about a bar mitzvah of a grandchild that took place in Jerusalem. Sure, it's expensive, but their son or daughter can afford it, thank God.

At first, Diana would point out that Jerusalem is a holy city, not only to the Jews, but to the Christians and the Arabs, as well. But, after this was met with several blank stares, and then some grumbling, she dropped that nugget from the stump speech.

Diana's also a little frustrated with the seeming inability of anyone to carry on an actual conversation, especially within my own family. She will be talking about some of the new research in gender-based communication, and they will counter with how cute I was as a baby. And what a good boy Stanley was!

I point out the fundamental mistake she's making.

"You're assuming that you're in an actual dialogue, which you're not. They know what they're going to say next, and nothing you say will influence that. They're just waiting for your lips to stop moving."

Once she accommodated herself to this idea, things got a little easier for her. She is incredibly patient with them, much more than I am, in truth. My father is, of course, the easiest for her to deal with. He is immediately smitten with Diana. It's actually more than that. Whatever comes after smitten. He credits Diana with the little "mini-recovery" in my life now. Me being back in school. Thinking about becoming a writer.

"Let's face it," he likes to say. "You were floundering before you met Diana."

There's a lot of evidence to support his position.

My father has a special role in the life of Century Village. He's younger than most of the people there, younger than all my grandma's relatives, by a lot. He's a big, strong guy, and he's basically responsible for all physical tasks—shopping, lifting, transporting, etc. He's their sturdiest warrior. The one they send out to meet the world. Their Agamemnon.

Interestingly, my grandmother gets all the credit for my dad's labors. One night, during a blinding rainstorm, my dad was dispatched, by my grandma, to pick up two of her cousins, Sissy and Sy, who were coming in at the airport that night. When they arrived at the apartment, ushered in by my dad, who was drenched from head to toe, Sissy hugged my grandma tight.

"Jenny, you shouldn't have," she said.

It was left to Diana to point out that Jenny actually hadn't.

"Shh," from my father.

Grandma has completely re-created her power base down here in Florida. She's surrounded herself with family members who adore her and are, in many cases literally, in her debt. With my father functioning as the Robert Duvall character in *Godfather,* or maybe more like Luca Brasi, she's firmly in control of her little corner of Century Village. No one walks by her front door without opening it and leaning in.

"You OK, Jenny? You need anything?"

Her standard reply: "George will get it."

Grandma was relatively young when my grandpa died in 1964. He had Parkinson's, and as that cruel disease progressed, Grandma would not let anyone else near him. She did everything. She fed him. She clothed him. She bathed him. She walked with him arm in arm around the block, her head held high, proud and strong. And she made him walk the same way.

"You didn't ask for this," she'd tell him. "You have nothing to be ashamed."

She has little time down here for widows who are dating and marrying again. Grandma does not recognize remarriage under any circumstance. A friend of hers, Helen Eisenberg, whose husband had died, had remarried recently. A charming man. Cultured. Very funny. We were all happy for Helen. One night at dinner, I was seated across the table from him.

"What's his name again?" I asked Grandma.

She looked over at him, looked back at me. "Second husband."

He wasn't the original model, and she wasn't going to bother learning his name. Grandma was still quite an attractive woman, and several of Grandpa's friends who had, sadly, lost their own wives, were quite obviously interested in her. Stanley and I tried to encourage her to entertain the idea.

"What about Abe Markovski, Grandma? He's such a nice man."

Grandma shuddered and spit on the ground.

"I had a husband," she told us.

And that was the end of that.

It's mind-numbingly hot in Florida. You actually begin to lose the ability to reason. We have a pass to the clubhouse and the pool, and we go down there every day with Shana. My dad has purchased for her every flotation device ever invented, and I enjoy watching them splash around together in the shallow end.

Diana and I sit and read by the pool's edge. We're often visited by Grandma's relatives or other neighbors. We try not to lose consciousness when forced to look at unending pictures of children and grandchildren. Pictures of their cars and of their homes. A couple of random, close-up shots of furniture.

"Sure, it's expensive where they live. But they can afford it, thank God."

The days at the pool end around three fifteen, when it's time to go back and dress for dinner. Have to hit that early bird special at four. And at Century Village, if you arrive late for dinner, say 4:01, you're going to have trouble getting a table.

At dinner, Diana's main goal is to try to get the family to not discuss cancer and other major surgical operations while we're eating. Diana points out one odd fact that I had never noticed. No one in my family is ever successfully operated on. Mostly, they're just "opened" and "closed."

"Uncle Morty, cancer of the liver. Opened him up, couldn't do a thing. Closed him right up. Pass the potatoes dear. Also, the same with Aunt Molly, Uncle Ben, and Cousin Shmilik. Opened and closed. More flanken, sweetheart?"

The person who's gotten lost in all this is my mother. Her health has been failing, and she's really just a shadow now of the super-energetic, super-intelligent, caustically funny woman I remember. For the most part, she just sits on the sidelines now, not really engaged.

Years later, after I'd become successful, I was visiting Century Village by myself. I saw a book on the living-room table, a popular novel of the day. I opened it, and on the inside was an inscription.

To Mom,

I owe it all to you.

Love,
Gary

I show her the inscription.
"I didn't write that, Mom."
She nodded.
"But that's how you feel. I know."

1985

{ chapter thirteen }

*B*eing the writer-producer of a hit television show, the kind done live in front of a studio audience, has to be the greatest job ever invented. I remember running into Jim Brooks on the Paramount lot, after he had just won three Academy Awards for *Terms of Endearment,* which he had written, directed, and produced.

"What was that like?" I asked him.

"It was great," he said. "Just great." And then he paused. "But, it's not like having a hit show."

People start lining up on Gower Street two nights early now, to wait for tickets to the show. Families write in and tell us that they're planning their vacation out to California around the availability of tickets to *Family Ties.* Michael Fox is receiving more mail than anyone else in the United States.

On stage, it seems, it's no longer simply a creative experience. It's become, somehow, a cultural event. When Mike is introduced before the show, the audience rises, screaming and stomping and clapping. Young girls are literally vibrating, yelling out his name.

The work itself is judged by entirely different standards, too, it seems. If Alex comes out and says hello, he gets a laugh. If he delivers an actual joke, we have to stop the show. We get three laughs when we deserve only one. Two laughs when we don't deserve any.

One of the tensions that develops on any successful series, and one we're dealing with now, is how to maintain a balance between what the audience needs and wants, which is basically what they've seen before, what they've come to love and expect—mention the word *money* and cut to a close-up of Alex. At the same time, find a way to provide ourselves what we need as writers and actors, to sustain us and grow creatively. To satisfy that ritual audience hunger, but somehow not fall into a trap of being repetitive and safe.

We're fortunate in that the basic setup for our show, a family unit, involves very natural patterns of growth and development. Alex is now in college; Mallory's in high school; Jennifer's a preteen. This allows new elements to be naturally introduced.

I like the idea of adding new writers each year. Preferably from other disciplines, preferably with no prior experience. This forces us to constantly reevaluate what we're doing and how we're doing it. Also, it gives us a chance to see our "world" again, through fresh eyes. And, it reminds us just how great this job is and how lucky we are to have it.

This year we've added Bruce Helford, a fugitive from the advertising world. Sue Borowitz off the *Harvard Lampoon.* And Katie Ford, a young playwright from Canada.

Bruce will go on to create *Drew Carey* and *George Lopez.* Sue, along with her husband Andy, will create *The Fresh Prince of Bel-Air.* And Katie will become producer of *Desperate Housewives,* as well as a successful screenwriter.

As always, our best episodes seem to come from our own lives. So, when Meredith Baxter does, in fact, become pregnant in real life, we see it as a great opportunity to expand our horizons creatively. (As well as a blessed event for Meredith, whom we all adore.)

The birth, on our show, of baby Andrew opens a whole new area of conflict and comedy for us. The battle between Steven and Elyse, Andrew's parents, and Alex, his beloved older brother, for preeminence in Andrew's life. What we call the "battle for Andrew's soul."

With Andrew's first line of dialogue, the battle lines are drawn. Steven, Elyse, and Alex are in the kitchen when the incredibly cute four-year-old Andrew, played by Brian Bonsall, peeks his head in. He's dressed like a little Alex—sweater vest, sports jacket, and tie.

"Alex come quick," he says excitedly. "Gold closed at 415." And he ducks back into the living room.

Michael Fox does a shameful thirty-second Jack Benny deadpan right into the camera and then turns to his parents. "Thank you for having him."

The first night that Brian Bonsall worked, everything was going very smoothly. We had finished five scenes, big laughs, and we were about to do the sixth and final scene, except nobody could find Brian. The audience had already been waiting half an hour, and we looked everywhere on stage but couldn't find him.

Finally, we locate him out in the parking lot, where he's crying and arguing with his mother, Kathy, because he wants to go home. He's changed out of his "Andrew" clothes, which he didn't like at all. It seems very few four-year-olds like wearing a sports jacket and tie. Who knew? And Brian has had it with being an actor.

I'm in the parking lot, trying to convince him to come back in and finish the show. But I don't have a lot of leverage. Most four-year-olds are immune to "you'll never work in this town again."

I do have one ace up my sleeve, though. My younger daughter Cailin, Brian's age, is in the audience. She's his friend, and I ask her to go talk to him and find out what's going on.

Cailin comes back with the scoop. Brian has a new Hawaiian shirt, which Michael Fox has bought for him. And if we let Brian wear that shirt in the final scene, he will come back in and finish the show.

From a script point of view, we have no way to explain the sudden switch to a Hawaiian motif. But we really have no choice. "Let's do it," I say. "I'll handle all the mail." Brian comes back on stage in Hawaiian splendor, and we finish the final scene. We did not get a single letter about the shirt.

Brian Bonsall does, in fact, idolize Michael Fox. Michael has gone out of his way to welcome Brian to the cast. Spent time with him off the set. Really tried to be his big brother. You can notice in most scenes, when they're together, Alex always has his hands on Andrew, in a show of brotherly affection. And every once in awhile, if you watch closely, you can notice Alex giving Andrew a little brotherly squeeze on his neck. However, that's not true brotherly love. At least, not completely. That was what Michael and Brian had worked out as Brian's cue as to when he was to speak. A little squeeze on the neck and Brian knew "my line now."

In the middle of the year, Steven Spielberg calls. They are in deep trouble on *Back to the Future,* and Steven's calling to ask for my help. Mike Fox had been the original choice for the part of Marty McFly. But the film's shooting schedule was so inflexible that, even though we wanted to make Mike available for them, we would have had to virtually shut down *Family Ties* in order to make that happen.

They began filming *Back to the Future* with another actor, but after about two months and several million dollars, they didn't feel they were getting what they needed. Steven was calling to see if there was any possible way now, halfway finished with our season, that we could free Mike up and allow him to take over the part of Marty.

I first met Steven in 1979, when we were introduced by my old college friend Kathy Kennedy. Even back in college, we all knew there was going to be no stopping Kathy. She was working then as Steven's assistant, where her intelligence, creativity, and incredible work ethic would quickly propel her to the very top ranks of film producers.* Steven had asked Kathy if she knew of any young writers who were good and fast and—perhaps most important— cheap. "I know one guy," Kathy told him. With my "credentials" firmly established, Steven hired me to write a screenplay for him— "Reel to Reel."

The movie was loosely based on the life of a young director very much like Steven, getting his first film job. The "research" I did

---

E.T. the Extra-Terrestrial, Indiana Jones and the Temple of Doom, Schindler's List, and *Seabiscuit,* among other huge hits.

required my shadowing Steven for weeks at a time. And over the course of that intense contact, was born the beginning of what would become, for me, a long, enduring, and extremely satisfying friendship.

When I finished my first draft of the script for him, Steven was in London, filming *Raiders of the Lost Ark.* And he brought me and Diana and Shana over to England, so I could work with him there.

I would visit him during the day on the *Raiders* set, and we would go over my "Reel to Reel" script between scenes. I loved the way he worked. Open to all ideas. Generous with his praise. Gentle with his criticisms. I would then go back to my room and work on those revisions. In the evening, when he was done shooting *Raiders* for the day, we would meet at his hotel and continue our work on "Reel to Reel."

"OK, where were we?" Steven would begin.

And he would then proceed to pick up the conversation we had been having several hours ago, exactly where we had left off, almost mid-sentence. This after a full day directing a very complicated major motion picture. I remember thinking, *OK, I get it. This guy's just smarter than the rest of us.*

Steven was the first person to see the rough-cut pilot of *Family Ties,* back in '82. We stood side by side in my living room and watched the show. When it was over, he turned to me and said, "It's a hit. I guarantee it. And that boy will be a major star." That first year, when the ratings were shaky, I was tempted to call Steven and ask him what exactly he meant by the term *guarantee.*

Steven thought they had come up with a plan now that could work for both of us. What they had decided was to basically shoot *Back to the Future* at night and on weekends. Mike could continue on *Family Ties* during the day, and of course we'd have him Friday night for the show. But after the show, instead of heading over to St. Germain, Mike would head over to Universal and film the movie. It was a daunting schedule, but my first instinct was to say yes.

I had two conditions. First, obviously, I wanted to make sure

Mike really wanted to take this on. But I was fairly certain that he did. And second, I wanted Mike to always have someone drive him to and from Paramount and Universal and whatever location they'd be on. Mike was already in his "I can go as fast as I want in my Ferrari and never get a ticket" phase, and the thought of him driving himself late at night and tired was not one that made me comfortable. But I really wanted him to get the chance to do this movie. I love both these guys very much, and I wanted to do everything I could to help make it happen.

I asked Mike to come read the script that Steven had sent over. It was all still secret at this point, and Mike had to read the script right there in my office while a messenger waited outside to take it back to Universal when he was done. Mike read it, getting more excited by the moment. My office was almost too small to contain the smile that was spreading across his face. When he finished, he closed the script and looked over at me. "You gotta be kiddin'!"

After Mike signed to do the film, I received phone calls from a few of my show-business-savvy friends telling me I'd made a terrible mistake, that I should never have allowed Mike to do this movie. "You didn't have to let him do that. You don't need it. Your show's doing great. The kid's gonna become a big film star, and then he's gonna quit your show."

These were knowledgeable men, too. Older. Wiser.

"Did I just make a terrible mistake?" I asked Diana.

She didn't hesitate.

"No. They don't know Michael, that's all. He would never do that."

And then, in an example of what puts Diana on a higher plane: "Anyway, we don't want to succeed if it means keeping someone else down."

"We don't?"

"No. If the price of the success of *Family Ties* is having to keep someone like Mike from being able to take advantage of this opportunity, then we'll just have to find some other way to be successful."

Of course, Mike didn't leave. And anytime he was questioned

about how long he would stay with *Family Ties,* he would say, "You know, Gary gave me the chance to do the movie. And I'll do the show as long as he wants me to."

Diana was right. They didn't know Mike.

There's one more gift waiting for Michael Fox this year. And it's going to be a gift whose worth will be beyond measure.

The new creative element to be added this year will be a love interest for Alex—the character of Ellen. She will be an artist. A feminist. The last person Alex would have ever expected to fall in love with. We wanted to show that even Alex Keaton, master of the universe in his own mind, is as helpless as the rest of us mortals when it involves affairs of the heart.

Judith Wiener hands me a tape of a young New York actress, Tracy Pollan. Tracy is well accomplished and respected. But, I almost don't fly her out, because it's too expensive. The studio is sure we can find who we need from the pool of available actors in Los Angeles.

But looking at Tracy's work on tape, there is something about her that intrigues me. She's a strikingly pretty young woman but seemingly unaffected and quite comfortable with it. She's such an honest actress. So real. This is going to be an important character for us. I want Mike to work with the best. And it seems we should at least fly Tracy out to L.A. and have Mike read with her.

We're down to our two final choices for the role of Ellen. Tracy and Deborah Foreman, an actress I like a lot, who has just starred in a very successful low-budget film, *Valley Girl.* I ask Mike to come over to my office and to read some sample scenes with both Deborah and Tracy.

Mike, as is his style, is enormously generous to both actresses. Tries to put each one at ease, is playful and helpful and totally charming and engaged. Really trying to put each actress in a position where she can show her best stuff. After we're done, I ask Mike if he has a preference.

"No. I like them both," he says.

"I do too," I tell him. "But I think I give the edge to Tracy Pollan. There's just something there I find incredibly compelling."

"Hey, it's your show. I'm OK either way. No big deal."

Four beautiful children and twenty happily married years later . . . Go plan a life.

1975

{ c h a p t e r   f o u r t e e n }

*O*n Memorial Day, we hitch a U-Haul up to the bumper of a very old VW Bug and head up to Los Angeles, seeking fame, fortune, and a Ph.D. in communication from USC. Diana has been looking over city maps and checking housing rentals in the paper, and she's circled a few neighborhoods and potential places for rent that she thinks might be promising.

"I think we should live on the river," she says, pointing on the map to a blue ribbon marked L.A. River, which snakes through the valley and into downtown. I like that idea. Maybe a little bungalow on the shore. I could put a table out back. Work to the sounds of the rushing water at my feet. Ubu can catch fish. Nice to be surrounded by nature.

"Yeah, that sounds like fun. Let's live on the river."

The only problem being that there is no L.A. River. It's an ugly, barren, concrete storm drain, chain-link fenced on all sides, surrounded by freeways. Maybe during Noah's time there was a trickle of water in there, but it's bone dry now.

Plan B, which we quickly put into effect, calls for us to find a place near USC. Maybe in the Highland Park area of older homes and neighborhoods. We find an actual house, or at least half a house, with a nice fenced yard for Ubu and a separate room for Shana. It's within our budget, and it seems like a great deal. We're surprised the house is so cheap.

That night we hear the gunfire. We're in the middle of gang territory, and all night long we hear cars screeching and loud voices screaming back and forth, and occasionally gunshots. "We do have the fenced yard," Ubu points out, looking for the silver lining. He's such a Labrador.

Somehow, we manage to settle in and settle down. Diana loves USC. Loves the people. Loves the program. It's a perfect fit. I practice calling her Doctor Meehan. It's very sexy. We find a day-care center for Shana within walking distance, and there's a nice park, not too far away, where Ubu and I can play Frisbee. We have to stay inside at night and keep all the doors and windows locked, but we're doing OK, and we do have the fenced yard.

I continue to turn out at least one spec script a week. The idea is not to actually sell those scripts to the respective shows—that almost never happens—but to generate enough interest in the material to make those producers want to call you in to pitch ideas for their shows, and maybe get an actual paying assignment. So far, Jim Preminger's gotten turned down everywhere, but people have been "incredibly polite," which we both take as a good sign.

Then we get our first nibble. Bernie West, of Nicholl, Ross and West (who would later create *Three's Company*), has read and liked my spec pilot "Free Clinic," which was based on time I spent volunteering at the clinic up in Berkeley. They're inviting me to come in and pitch ideas for their new show *The Dumplings,* starring Geraldine Brooks and James Coco.

What was fascinating about Nicholl, Ross and West (aside from their willingness to meet with me) was that they functioned in communication terms as a classic three-person problem-solving group. Diana, going for her Ph.D. in communication, was becoming something of an expert in the field of small-group communication in general and three-person problem-solving groups in particular—the workings of which, she felt confident, she could predict.

The first order of business was to organize and position my story ideas for maximum impact. Evidently there is an ebb and flow to

129

the dynamics of any small-group meeting, and there are specific "moments" in those meetings, when participants are more "available" to good ideas. What you want to do, obviously, is try to have your best ideas being pitched at those most propitious moments. In my presentation, the stars aligned at story ideas number two and number seven.

As for the dynamics of the group itself, basically all three-person problem-solving groups operate in the same way. In lay terms, Diana explained, they represent the "heart," the "blood," and the "mind," with each of the partners playing one of those roles.

When I nervously began to pitch my first idea, it became immediately clear that Bernie West was going to be the heart. Whatever idea I threw out, he loved it. He supported it. It was great. I was great.

Mickey Ross was the blood. He took the idea that Bernie and I loved and pumped it up, kept it flowing, supplied "nutrients" and "oxygen," in the form of story turns and characters that could be added.

Don Nicholl was the mind. He said yes or no, and "What else do you have?" He said whether or not they would buy it.

There was some overlap, of course, but mostly they stayed within those roles, and it was all I could do to not jump up and shout, "You guys are a sketch three-person problem-solving group, and I love you for it." And when Don Nicholl bought my second idea, and then bought my seventh, Bernie hugged me, and Mickey immediately thought of ten different ways to make them better.

Outside the KTTV building on Sunset Boulevard, there's a rack of pay phones, and I stop to call Diana. She's screaming, and I can almost see her jumping up and down. Ubu's barking excitedly in the background, and I can hear her telling him what happened. That night we have a few people over to celebrate. I've bought lox for the occasion, which is what I think wealthy people serve at these kinds of events. There's cream cheese, too, and bagels, of course. Chopped liver, some knishes. It's a mini–bar mitzvah.

Jim Preminger comes up. He's all smiles, and he has some papers for me to sign. I feel very important. I've never signed any papers before, and this seems to make it official. Upon signing, I'll receive $1,000. Another $1,850 when I hand in the first draft. And $1,850 for the second. A total of $4,700. I make a note to purchase life insurance.

Diana calls Jack and Brenda. I call my parents and my brother. I call Nate Monaster. Diana calls her Aunt Rosemary. I start calling people at random out of the phone book.

Bernie West had said to have the script in on Monday, and I didn't know he was kidding, so I work all weekend to finish the first draft. When I show up at their offices on Monday, they're so surprised and, I guess, a little guilty, that they ask me to wait outside, and they're going to read it right now.

After an hour, Bernie and Mickey come back out. They really like the script. I don't need to do a second draft, although I will get paid for it. They want me to get started right away on the second idea I had sold to them. If I want, I can even take three days to write this one.

I write the second script fairly quickly too, and hand it in. Again, everybody there seems to like it, and they invite me to hang around and be "on staff," but not really, since they don't have any extra money, and I won't actually get paid.

Jim Preminger is not happy. He doesn't think I should do this if I'm not officially getting paid.

To me, this seems like a great trade-off. My time and energy for their expertise. It's the old Berkeley barter system. And maybe, on some level, I feel less pressure, since I won't actually be getting paid. I look at it as a fellowship.

I tell Jim, "Look, this is either the start of a very long career, in which case, what's the difference? Or, it's the last job I'll ever have, in which case, what's the difference?"

They set up a desk for me in the hall, and I get to work. Basically, my job is to punch up scenes that are structurally sound from a storytelling point of view but might need a few more jokes. Sometimes they'll just give me an area or a setting. A doctor's office, two former lovers meet at a clown convention. It didn't matter to me. I was so excited, I could barely keep up with my pen.

The hours were long and the pay literally nonexistent, but it was everything I could have dreamed of—except for one thing: A lot of the jokes and moments I cared most about were not getting into the final scripts. Bernie and Mickey seemed to respond best to what I thought were actually the weaker and more obvious jokes I was turning out, and to reject what I thought were the better elements of my work. In any case, it was a different kind of comedy than I dreamed of doing.

After about three weeks, Bernie told me how happy they were with my work. And that it looked like there would be some money available soon for me to come on as a staff writer and actually get paid—$850 dollars a week.

That night, sitting around with Diana and Ubu, I'm not happy. I'm having a "career crisis." Three weeks ago, I didn't have a career; now I have one, and it has a crisis.

"I don't think I can take the job."

"Why not?"

"These guys are so great, but we have really fundamentally different ideas about what's funny. It's painful to be in a room where everyone is laughing except you. It actually hurts physically."

"So, don't take it, then."

"It's eight hundred and fifty dollars a week."

"So what?"

Ubu's not sure. Labradors can be incredibly conservative financially.

"We need the money," I tell Diana.

"We need you to be happy," she tells me.

And that would always be her position. Whether it was $850 I was offered, or $8,500, or $850,000, Diana's advice would always be the same. "Don't do it if you're not happy."

I go in to see Bernie and Mickey. I explain to them how grateful I am. They gave me my first job, and I'll love them forever. And I want to be able to take this job. I really do. I mean, I have food stamps in my pocket and a family at home, but the differences in sensibility are difficult to reconcile. And my biggest fear is that I will disappoint them. That I won't be able to provide the kind of comedy they're looking for. So I have to say no.

They are incredibly gracious and don't seem to take offense.

"What about MTM?" Bernie says, referring to the Mary Tyler Moore company, known for a more sophisticated type of comedy.* "That might be a good place for Gary."

"Yeah, MTM," Mickey agrees. "That might be OK."

They call over to MTM on my behalf and send copies of my *Dumplings* first drafts over there as well. Eventually, the scripts make their way over to the *Newhart* people, Gordon and Lynne Farr, who are the story editors for Tom Patchett and Jay Tarses, the producers and head writers. Gordon and Lynne respond well and call me in to pitch. This is like being called up to the major leagues, and I need to make sure I'm ready.

I prepare twenty-six story ideas for my meeting with the Farrs. Not just vague notions and outlines, either—full stories with act breaks and dialogue. I doodle set designs and costume sketches, I write some alternate theme songs, and when I drive over to CBS Radford for the meeting, even though I'm eleven hours early, I'm feeling pretty good about myself.

The Farrs could not be more welcoming and supportive. They say how much they liked my scripts. I tell them what a big fan of the show I am, which is true. We pour coffee and tea, and I get out my notebook of ideas. Evidently, no one has ever come in with twenty-six ideas, so I immediately win "Most Eager."

The first six ideas I pitch, including one where Jerry the dentist learns he's adopted and one where the receptionist Carol's boyfriend,

---

The Mary Tyler Moore Show, The Bob Newhart Show, Rhoda.

Larry Bondurant, opens a travel agency in Bob's office building, are ideas that they've already decided they want to do this upcoming season. (Which I could have had no way of knowing). Tom Patchett and Jay Tarses come in and say hi, and now I'm in a room with the four funniest people I've ever met. I'm trying to remember everything they're saying, so I can share it later with Diana.

I make a sale. An episode where Carol, Bob's secretary, feels overworked and overlooked and quits. They like it. They've been wanting to develop more for that character this year—and there it is. I'm going to write an episode of *The Bob Newhart Show.* Bob Newhart! I love Bob Newhart. I have all his albums. I love his show. I love the Farrs, I love Tom and Jay, I love MTM, I love the cat that meows at the end of every episode (forgive me, Ubu). The door to the candy store has been pushed wide open, and they're inviting me to step inside.

1985

{ c h a p t e r   f i f t e e n }

The Facts of Life has gone to Paris to make a TV movie. And for some unknown reason this has upset me. I like *The Facts of Life*. I like the girls. I think Nancy McKeon is a major talent and a lovely person. And yet, I seem to be annoyed by this little Parisian jaunt of theirs.

I call Brandon Tartikoff.

"If *Facts of Life* can do a TV movie in Europe, so can we."

"OK."

"And we're going to go someplace where I speak the language. We're going to London."

"OK. What's the movie going to be about?"

"I don't know."

"OK."

With little more thought than that, I launch our team off on an adventure that will be grueling, joyless, and confusing. And, will produce a lamentable piece of television fare, imaginatively entitled *The Family Ties Movie*.

My motives weren't simply pettiness and jealously, although those were the dominant, driving forces. I liked the idea of stretching our creative muscles. Trying a different form. Longer. On film. No audience. Also, I naïvely thought it would be fun. Kind of a reward for all the hard work we'd been doing. And a chance to celebrate our success with a European flavor. But let's not forget pettiness and jealously.

136

We start with a few, simple ideas. Alex will go to Oxford for summer study. A prince will fall in love with Mallory. At one moment in the film, Steven and Alex will have to wear those fluffy English judicial wigs. That sounds like a reason to do a movie right there.

Basically it's going to be a spy-comedy-thriller, centering around microfilm hidden in a hairbrush, which is mistakenly picked up by Jennifer and put in her suitcase. As it will turn out, our work will be neither comedic nor thrilling. But we don't know that yet. We optimistically break up the story, such as it is, into the four-act movie-of-the-week structure. And then Alan Uger, Michael Weithorn, Marc Lawrence, and I go off separately, to each write one act.

When we reconvene and put the acts together, they don't quite mesh. And there are at least five separate moments in the script when not one of us can say where the hairbrush actually is located. This does not augur well.

I mention to Brandon that we're not thrilled with what we've done so far, but he seems unconcerned. *Back to the Future* is coming out in July, and he's planning to piggyback on that expected monster box-office success by opening up their fall season on NBC with our movie.

"You guys will pull it out, you always do."

"I don't know."

"You guys are great. It's going to be great. Have fun over there."

What happened to network interference? And where is it when you need some?

In London, we meet for the table read at the Churchill Hotel, where we're all staying. We've done some further work on the script, but it's still a little rough, to put it in the best possible light. And we begin to read.

After what feels like a week and a half later, we're done. There is stunned silence. Mike Fox looks up at me and shrugs.

"I'm going shopping."

I point out that, yes, a round of shopping is perhaps an appropriate response to this script. I recommend the entire cast go shopping. Perhaps tour the National Gallery. Take in a show. Hopefully there will be a different and better script here for them in the morning.

The writers all go up to my room, and we begin to rewrite. We work all through that day and into the night and into the early London morning fog, in what will become an all-too-familiar scene of too many scones, too much clotted cream, not enough good jokes.

What we're trying to accomplish, at this point, is to at least cobble together a coherent narrative to the movie. Ground our "spy-caper" story, which is much broader than our usual storytelling style, into something with which the actors can feel more comfortable. We're just trying to get them "through the door" for now. Trusting our ability to watch rehearsal and make the necessary adjustments on the set.

The problem is that the movie-making format will not allow us to make these adjustments. At least not on the scale we've become accustomed to. On stage 24, on a Tuesday, with a troubled show, it was not uncommon to simply throw that script out and start over again with an entirely new script and a new story on Wednesday morning.

But in the world of movie making, the script is broken down into scenes and shot out of order. And the task, primarily, is to get through that day's work on time. So, when we see a rehearsal of a scene, we're severely limited in what we can do to change it and make it better, without disrupting the schedule for the whole movie.

To compound things, we're shooting entirely on location. We only have these locations for a specific amount of time, so if we don't finish the day's work, we can't come back the next day. So the goal becomes finishing the scene. As opposed to making it better, which takes time, which we don't have.

It's hard for us to work this way. Whatever talent we bring to the process of making television comedy is really of little value here. We stand on the side of the set, scribbling furiously, only to be told we have to be quiet. They're shooting. What they're shooting's not great. But they're shooting.

One day we step outside to try to completely rewrite a scene that desperately needs to be completely rewritten. We duck into a little trailer, which is attached to a truck and parked off to the side next to the wardrobe trailer. We settle into the cramped space and furiously begin pitching ideas back and forth, when we hear a loud thud and we're all knocked sideways, papers and scripts flying off the little table. And now we're moving.

It seems no one noticed us getting into the trailer to write, and the driver is taking off for the next location. We're screaming and pounding, but no one can hear us back in our isolated, self-contained trailer. And as we get dragged off into the London countryside, it seems a fitting metaphor for this misadventure.

One other awkward aspect to this trip. *Back to the Future* was originally scheduled to open in September. And with our movie wrapping up in July, it seemed like it would be no problem to break Mike free to attend the gala opening in New York and bask in all the glamour and hoopla that comes with a major movie premiere. However, Amblin and Universal are so thrilled with the movie they now have, they've decided to push the premiere date up to the first week in July. And that means our *Family Ties* movie won't be finished filming in time for Mike to make the premiere.

Mike's being a good sport, but I know how disappointed he is. Steven and Kathy are not helping by sending telegrams about how great the reviews have been, how enthusiastic the studio is, etc. They're just excited, and I don't blame them. But the contrast between the energy surrounding the two projects is hard to reconcile.

On the day that *Back to the Future* premieres in the United States, to box-office records and rave reviews, Mike is stuck in the English countryside, shooting a scene where he's locked in a closet, in his underwear, bound and gagged. He's squashed between four elderly British actors, also bound, gagged, and in their underwear.

When the first take of the scene is over, Mike comes out gasping for air. The assistant director brings a telegram over for him. It's from Steven and Kathy, congratulating Mike and thanking him. And filling him in on the almost unprecedented glow that's surrounding the *Back to the Future* opening. Mike shows me the telegram. I smile and give him a hug. They call, "Places." Mike steps back into the closet to again be bound and gagged.

In September, NBC kicks off their fall season with *The Family Ties Movie.* And we are the highest rated show of the night, as Brandon felt sure we would be.

"What about Portugal, next year?" he asks me. "Or Spain? Maybe Mexico?"

"No, *gracias.*"

We've learned our lesson. We're going to hang around the kitchen table where we belong.

My parents and my grandma are coming out to visit. This will be their first trip to California and Grandma's first time ever in an airplane. The flight had gone fairly well, my father told me, until they hit some turbulence, outside of Chicago. The seat belt announcement was made, but Grandma did not want to comply. She didn't like the idea of being "locked in." The stewardess, a "Mary Tyler Moore type," according to my dad, comes over and asks Grandma very sweetly to put her seat belt on. Grandma says no.

"It's for your own safety, ma'am. The captain requests it. He's run into some turbulence."

Grandma shook her head. "Who told him to go this way?" A question, I'm sure, that was on the minds of a lot of other passengers at the same moment.

Anyway, they're here safely now, and Diana and I have gone to the airport to pick them up. The usual hugs and kisses and crying. I go to pick up one of the suitcases, and I can't move it. It weighs a thousand pounds.

"Jeez, this is heavy. What's in here?" I ask my dad.

"Tuna fish."

"What?"

"It's the kind you like. It was on sale, so I picked up a case for you."

"There's a case of tuna fish in here? Forty-eight cans?"

"No, not a whole case," he says, as if that would be the silliest thing in the world, "half."

Only twenty-four cans. Now it makes sense.

"Also, Grandma's frying pan is in there. She wants to make blintzes for you, and she wasn't sure you'd have the right pan."

Trying to show off and somehow repay them for all they went through with me, I've put them up in one of the finest hotels in Beverly Hills and have arranged for them to stay in the presidential penthouse suite, which is about five times the size of our apartment in Brooklyn and has a wraparound terrace, with ocean and city views. The problems start almost immediately. They're nervous about the "patio," my father confides, pointing to my mother and my grandmother.

"You could fall off."

"Not very likely," I tell them.

"We know someone in Florida who fell off and died."

"Who was that?"

"Harriet Bilawski's sister, her neighbor had a brother, married a girl from Queens, and that girl's sister's husband. It was his nephew who fell off."

"When it hits that close to home."

The door to the dangerous "patio" is sealed, which still leaves about 8,500 square feet of interior space, so I think we'll be OK.

Everyone's a little tired with "the jet lag." This is their first flight ever, but they are now experts on "the jet lag." We hug and kiss good-bye, and we'll see each other in the morning.

At my house, the phone rings at 5 A.M. It's my father.

"Where are you? We're waiting."

"It's five in the morning, Dad. It's still dark out."

He's sorry. They forgot about the time change. I hear them arguing in the background about whose fault it is. My father takes the blame. It's easier that way.

"I'll come over."

"No. Go back to sleep, boychik."

"It's OK. I'm already up. We'll get an early start to the day."

I show up at the hotel, and everyone is sitting there in the living room, fully dressed; they all have their coats on. My grandma's wrapped in a blanket. It's about minus-four degrees in the presidential suite.

"It's freezing in here. Why didn't you turn the air off?"

"We couldn't find it."

"Why didn't you call the front desk?"

"We don't want to be any trouble."

I find the thermostat and stabilize the temperature.

"So, everybody sleep well?"

"Nobody slept."

Evidently, my father kept going from room to room. "Why do we have this room? What are we supposed to do in here? Why do we need a library?"

This brings an end to the great Beverly Hills experiment. I move them to a small hotel in Santa Monica, the Oceana, where they have their own kitchen, and they can cook for themselves. They're happy again.

They all come out to Paramount to see my office. I have Lucille Ball's old dressing room, right next to Bing Crosby's former abode. This is almost too much for them to grasp—that I am sitting where Lucy sat, near where Bing crooned.

My father takes a picture of everything in my office. He takes a picture of my parking spot with my name on it. In the commissary, Henry Winkler comes by. Henry's a good friend and a sweet, sweet man. We hug, Henry does a lovely couple of minutes with my family, and then he goes.

"That's the Fonz," my father tells me.

"I know, Dad. Henry's a good friend."

"He's the Fonz."

My dad is enjoying show business more than anyone since talkies were invented. He tells me that he's worried about Brandon Tartikoff. I point out he's never met Brandon. Why is he worried out him?

"He's so young. All that pressure."

"He likes that pressure, Dad. It's exciting for him."

"It's too much."

He asks me a lot of questions about the NBC schedule. He's not sure about some of the moves they're making. Again, he tells me he's worried about Brandon.

"Why don't you call him, Dad?" I laugh. "Maybe you can help them fix their Friday night."

The afternoon's big event is a trip out to Burbank to see *The Johnny Carson Show*. I explain to my father that NBC has set aside special VIP tickets for him. When we get there, I'll drop them off in front, and he's to go around to the side door, the VIP door, and he's to say, "I'm George Goldberg, and you have special tickets for me." He's on it.

When we get to Burbank, the temperature's 143 degrees, and the line for tickets to the *Carson* show is stretching for about a mile and a half. Looks like people have been there for a while, too. And, as I drop them off, I tell my dad one last time, just to be sure.

"Don't get into that line, OK? The one where the people are passing out from sunstroke. Go around to the side. They have special tickets in your name. You'll be inside in the air-conditioned studio in two minutes."

"Got it," my dad says. "Don't worry."

I go to park the car, and when I come back, the line for *Carson,* if anything, has gotten longer. And there, at the very end of the line, are my father, my mother, and my grandmother. I understand. He just can't bring himself to go through a door marked VIP. To go up to anyone and say, "I'm George Goldberg, and you have special tickets for me."

I walk over to them. My father shrugs and smiles, a little embarrassed. I put my arm around him, and I give him a kiss. Then, I lead the three of them around the corner and knock on the door that says VIP. The door opens and we step inside.

Within two years my father will be dead. Lung cancer. He just could not give up smoking cigarettes. I think, if they had let him, he would have smoked while he was on the operating table. During the last years of his illness, he was mostly confined to a hospital bed, and either my brother or I was with him in Miami every weekend.

One Saturday, Stanley and I were down there together, and Dad was enjoying one of his very rare good days. We were laughing and telling stories. We remembered Stanley's first day as a teacher, when Dad insisted on driving him to work, because the school was over in Bushwick and there was a lot of construction in that area and a lot of one-way streets and Dad wasn't comfortable with Stanley trying to navigate that all by himself. Dad was going to drive him there, then take the subway back home by himself.

Unfortunately, with Dad behind the wheel, they were two and a half hours late. Dad getting not only one ticket that day, but two— one for going up a one-way street and the second one for the rarely seen 360-degree illegal U-turn, where Dad got confused and ended up going back the same way he had come.

We remembered the time of Grandpa's funeral, when Grandma wouldn't come down off the front stoop. She just stood there on the steps, holding on to the railing, crying and screaming. A wail from beyond this universe. Dad gently went to her, put his arm around her.

"C'mon, Ma, get into the hearse."

That didn't help get Grandma off the stoop.

He asked me about that check still waiting for me at the post office. I told him I'd think about it. But, as he knew, I *had* made a vow.

Dad smiled, nodding in a fond memory, looking for a moment almost like his old self—but just for one brief moment, and then it was gone. He looked up at us. Studying the faces of the men his two boys had become. He was so happy that Stanley and I had stayed so close. So proud of my brother, an assistant principal now and a successful camp owner in his own right.

It was late afternoon, and Dad was getting tired. As he leaned back, this formerly 6'2" man swallowed up now by the pillows and the blankets, he asked Stanley and me to come near the bed, and he took our hands in his, those once-mighty meat hooks, now ricepaper thin and cold. He looked at us and shrugged, almost embarrassed.

"You know, when I look at you two guys, I don't know, I must've done something right."

He closed his eyes and fell asleep. We left him there, and that was the last time we saw him alive. Those were his last words.

1976

{c h a p t e r s i x t e e n}

*T*hey've given me a tiny office on the MTM lot now, with a view of the CBS sign and a deal to write three episodes for *The Bob Newhart Show.* I have only one thought running through my head: It can't be possible to make a living like this. It's too much fun. At some point, someone's going to come in here, put their hand on my shoulder and tell me, "C'mon, get outta here. Who're you kiddin'?"

Being at MTM is like being at a small, very good men's college. There are a few talented females "on campus"—Lynne Farr, Pat Nardo, Gloria Banta, Charlotte Brown—but otherwise it's exclusively male at this time. In the hall, I rub shoulders with legends like James L. Brooks, Allan Burns, Ed. Weinberger. The best of the best, the Murderer's Row of comedy writers.* One day, Jim Brooks knows my name. I can't believe it.

"Morning, Larry," he says.

OK, not perfect, but very close. And he *is* Jim Brooks. Maybe Larry's funnier.

Grant Tinker is the force behind the elegant, intelligent comedies that are being written here. Fiercely protective of his writers and their autonomy, Grant has a rare genius for recognizing and nurturing talent. Charming, unassuming, unpretentious—the model

---

*Between them they've garnered thirty-nine Emmys for *Mary*, *Rhoda*, *Room 222*, and *The Johnny Carson Show*, among others.

of the perfect boss. MTM and its success reflect Grant's vision and his values.

Tom Patchett and Jay Tarses are, themselves, outrageously funny. Emmy winners for *The Carol Burnett Show*, they met as advertising guys in Lancaster, Pennsylvania and did stand-up together. While incredibly hostile toward each other and all network executives, they are kind and generous to me.

Their office, where we write, is not a typical office. It's actually a re-creation of Tom's kitchen back in Lancaster, complete with a replica of the kitchen table where Tom and Jay sat and wrote their own spec scripts when they first started out. It's also emblematic of who they are. Unconcerned with the trappings of power, they seem indifferent to their rise to the top of the Hollywood food chain.

They allow me to sit in on story meetings and on rewrites, even on some casting sessions. I'm in awe of their talent and their ability to juggle all the different roles. But mostly I'm in awe of how funny they are. At the end of the day I find myself literally sore from laughing. "No pain, no gain," I remember.

Because of how deliriously happy I am, I become a source of amusement for Tom and Jay. They start calling me "John-Boy," after the earnest Richard Thomas character on *The Waltons*. Any really annoying thing that has to be done, any truly unpleasant chore, they give to me.

"Let John-Boy do it. He doesn't mind."

The truth is, I *don't* mind. Maybe because I'm older. Maybe because I've been so broke and done so many bad jobs for so little money. Maybe because I've been on food stamps for so long I didn't know they actually took money in grocery stores. Maybe because I can come to work in shorts and a T-shirt, and play tennis with these guys at lunch and softball with them on the weekends. Or maybe because I'm laughing 90 percent of my waking hours, but there is nothing about this job that I don't love.

It's now the night of the filming of my *Newhart* episode, "*Et Tu, Carol*," based on the idea I pitched that day in the room with Gordon and Lynne Farr. I've been involved in the rewrites all along, but at this point there's probably only 3 percent of my original writing still left. I have to admit, they've made it better.

I have had no interaction with any of the cast members, although one time Suzanne Pleshette catches me staring at her, amazed by how beautiful she is, and she smiles at me and waves. I can't believe I've actually written sentences that Bob Newhart will say. Or I guess it's down to scattered words now. Or *a* word.

Diana's parents, Jack and Brenda, come down for the filming. We're much more comfortable and close with each other now. And they are my biggest fans. Shana helps a lot. She's so obviously a happy and healthy toddler. And so loving.

The show goes well. When the first joke I wrote gets a big laugh from the audience, it's all I can do to not run out on the set and hug Newhart and yell, "I wrote that joke. That was me."

After the show, Diana and I take Brenda and Jack out for dinner to the Cock 'n' Bull, on Ventura Boulevard. It's a real '50s throwback place. Deep leather banquettes, dark woods, healthy drinks. The kind of place where you have a choice of meat or other meat. It seems like the kind of place you go after your first show. Maybe light a cigar, too? And I experience that special thrill I always get when I walk into a restaurant and I'm not the one having to wait on tables.

As it turns out, Bob Newhart is also there with his wife Ginny, as well as Suzanne Pleshette and her husband, Tom Gallagher. Brenda wants us to go over and say hi.

"He'll be excited to see you. The writer of his show. He probably doesn't know you're here."

He probably doesn't know I exist, I'm thinking, but Brenda, and now Jack, really want to go over and say hi. They're so proud of me. There's no way they can let this moment pass, and by the way, they want to get a picture, too.

"With Bob," Brenda says.

"And Suzanne," Jack adds, sounding a little whiny for a World War II pilot. "Let's not forget Suzanne."

When we reach the Newhart table, I'm not quite sure exactly what I'm going to say, but I start with "Hi, Bob," which is what I figure I would say if I actually did know him. Or had ever met him. Bob looks up from his meat. There's kindness mixed with the confusion in his eyes.

"Gary Goldberg." I offer my hand, and he takes it warily, and we shake.

"The writer," Brenda offers proudly, suddenly a Jewish mother.

I don't have to worry too much about Jack at this point. Being in close proximity to Suzanne Pleshette, he's lost the ability to speak. I introduce Brenda and a smiling Jack to everyone, explaining that they're my in-laws and they came down from Santa Cruz to watch the filming of the show I wrote. And now Newhart gets it, and, God bless him, he is instantly on board and proceeds to deal with me as if I was Anton Chekhov. What a pleasure it was to speak my dialogue. How lucky they are to have me on the staff. My mother-in-law is beaming. My father-in-law, although still catatonic, manages a nod and smile. We walk back to our table.

"See," Brenda says. "How hard was that?"

The next two scripts I write for *Newhart* seem to go well, and I'm starting to get a little bit of a "name" for myself out there, Jim Preminger reports. Arnie Kane at Universal hires me to do an episode of *Alice*. Then Ed. Weinberger hires me to do an episode of *Phyllis*, the *Mary* spin-off he's producing for CBS. Patchett and Tarses also have a new show for next season starring Tony Randall, and they hire me to be the story editor, along with another young protégé of theirs, Hugh Wilson. Hugh will go on to create *WKRP in Cincinnati* and direct the *Police Academy* movies, but for now this is his first staff job too.

Diana and I move to Santa Monica, where there's a lot less gunfire, and we buy a car. This will be the first actual new car either of us has ever purchased in our lives, and in a mini-homage to our trip out west in '72, we buy a Ford LTD. We're so nervous about the scale of the purchase, however, that at the last minute we pull back and order the car without power steering. We save $425 but lose the ability to parallel park. And you need at least three hands on the wheel to make a left turn. They call it power steering for a reason! Tom Patchett comes down to the parking lot to see the LTD. He looks at it, turns to me: "There are better cars in your future."

The first year of *The Tony Randall Show* does not go smoothly at all. For one thing, Tom and Jay are not speaking to each other. And they're certainly not speaking to anyone at the network. They refuse to take Fred Silverman's calls. When I point out that he is the head of ABC and perhaps the most important person in network television, they seem unimpressed. "Why don't you call him, John-Boy?" Jay tells me. "You like him so much."

"I'd be happy to call him, but he won't talk to me."

"If he won't talk to you, then we won't talk to him."

The other serious problem is that Tom and Jay are not getting along with Tony Randall. Tony would like to have a lot more input, and Tom and Jay are very resistant to that idea. I'm torn. On the one hand, my loyalties are to Tom and Jay. They've given me my break. On the other hand, I completely sympathize with Tony's point of view. I've come to admire him a great deal. He's very smart, really understands the type of comedy that works for him, and he has a lot at stake here in terms of his own career and prestige.

"What's the name of this show again?" Tony likes to ask, holding up a copy of the script. "Oh, look, it's *The Tony Randall Show*! And I'm Tony Randall. Shouldn't I have something to say?"

At the end of the first season, even though we have a 27 share, the show is canceled. Fred Silverman's way of showing his unhappiness with the way he was treated, perhaps.

"A very small man," Jay intones.

Grant Tinker, in a brilliant stroke, convinces CBS to pick up the show, and we're given a full order for twenty-four new episodes. Tony though, has one condition for returning. He doesn't want to work with Tom and Jay. That's not a big problem for them; they get paid anyway. And with everyone protecting their own positions, and firmly believing that I, as the lowest man on the totem pole, as the one person they can most easily control, seeing me as a complete figurehead without any power, a complete cipher whom they can all manipulate, it's decided, that I, along with Hugh Wilson, will be moved up to Producer.

I run into Allan Burns in the hall. "Hey, congratulations. I hear you've been moved up to producer."

"Thank you."

"How long have you been in the business, anyway?"

"Altogether, almost eighteen months."

Allan stares at me for a beat.

"Gee. Sorry it took so long."

The only one who's not as deliriously happy is Ubu. I mean, he's happy for my success, obviously. But the new professional demands on me, and on Diana, have kind of reduced his paw print in the world.

In the beginning, I was able to take him with me to work at least three times a week. The old Radford lot was where they used to shoot *Gunsmoke.* Ubu and I would walk down the main street in Dodge City together, me lookin' for Marshal Dillon and Miss Kitty, Ubu lookin' for kitties of a different stripe.

There was also the *Gilligan's Island* set on the back lot for us to explore. We'd romp around on the island. Occasionally, one of us would chase a stick or swim after a Frisbee.

But now the Radford lot is under big development, and our old haunts are being bulldozed for office buildings. They've also instituted a leash law. While Ubu has no problems with the idea of a leash, per se, he doesn't understand why I get to be the one who holds it.

Back home in Santa Monica, the walls are moving in on us as well. Our apartment building's under new management, and pets are no longer allowed. We're in a bit of a bind here, since we love this neighborhood and we're within walking distance of Shana's school.

I see the confusion in Ubu's eyes when he drops the Frisbee at my feet, and I tell him, "I can't play now. I have to work." He walks back across the living room, tail hanging low, not wagging at all. "What'd I do wrong?"

I realize how, in the past, so much of my life was always happily devoted just to playing with him. Making sure he got out to the park. Making sure he got his half-hour belly-rub in the morning. How much I loved just to be with him. To just hang out. To be best friends. But not anymore.

Then, out of the blue, we get a call from our old friends Mike Ackerman and Barb VanSickle, asking if we would consider sending Ubu out to them for a visit. We met Mike and Barb, in Greece in '72, when they gave us the greatest ride we were ever able to thumb—three weeks in Crete with them, living out of their VW van.

As we moved up into the colder mountain areas of Crete, Ubu would wait with me and Diana to see if we would be putting up our little orange tent, or if we were just going to sleep outside in our sleeping bags. If we didn't put up the tent, Ubu would start out with us, for appearance's sake and out of some sense of Labrador loyalty. But when it got too cold, he would go over and scratch at the door of the van, and Mike and Barb would let him in to sleep with them. In bed. Under the covers.

Mike and Barb are really Ubu's second family, and what they're offering is very appealing. They live on a commune in the Ozark Mountains. And the idea of Ubu running free in the Missouri hills, in the company of Mike and Barb, whom he loves, makes for a satisfying picture.

We agree to send him on a visit. We're sending him to "camp" is how we rationalize it to ourselves. It's better for him, but it's crushing for us.

On the day we're going to send him, I'm such a coward, I can't even get out of bed. To my everlasting shame, Diana has to take him to the airport herself. On some level, I know he won't come back. That the life there is going to be too perfect for him. That it will be better for him there.

We get letters, and pictures of Ubu, from Mike and Barb. Ubu's a hero in the Ozarks. He serves as a messenger for outlying communes and neighbors who don't have phones. They attach notes to Ubu's collar and send him over the hill.

"Go take this to Peter Good Vibe's Farm," they tell him, and off he goes to deliver the message. Tail held high.

He'll live to be fourteen, Ubu. He'll have puppies and grand-puppies and become a mythical figure in the world of Ozark hippie lore. He'll never be on a leash. He'll learn to bark at the TV when his picture comes on and he hears my voice. And then he'll sit, like the good dog he is. But we'll never see him again.

I know it was better for him. I know he was happier there. I know that was the life that he deserved. But . . .

My only real regret in life. My only one.

1987

{ chapter seventeen }

*T*he UBU Empire is in full bloom. Run by two talented executives, Mitch Semel and Jay Fukuto, the company has several television shows on the air at the same time. We have a movie company in place, run by Ruth Vitale. We have our own head of production, Paul Heller. We have our own building on the Paramount lot.

I travel back and forth across town visiting the sets of our different series. I have a stretch limousine and a driver, and in between visits to the shows, I sit in the back and look at video tapes, make notes. Read scripts. I'm a mogul. But not a very good one. Or a very happy one.

For one thing, I get nauseous trying to read or watch TV in a moving vehicle. So I usually arrive on the set having not completed my work, and a little dizzy. For another, I barely have a chance anymore to do any writing of my own. Mostly, all I do is comment on, and make notes on, other people's writing. And I don't enjoy that role.

I'm not comfortable telling other writers what to do on their own shows. Even shows that are for my company. And I find myself giving notes like "Move the story up." Or "Hang a lantern on it." "Raise the stakes." And other gems, like "Can't this be better?"

The cast of *Family Ties,* although they've been great and joke about it, on some level resent the time I spend away from the *Ties* set. They refer to my visits to the "O.S." (other shows), as if they

158

were women and I was carrying on a series of affairs. I think I feel like that myself a little too. That I'm being unfaithful to my true love.

At the other shows, I'm a more distant figure. Someone they feel they have to please, rather than someone they work together with on the same team. Not the coach, anymore, but the general manager. Or the owner.

The fact that the "Empire" exists at all is based, primarily, on the success of our flagship show, *Family Ties.* But it's also due to a battle of incompetence that was waged between the business-affairs guys at Paramount and their counterparts at NBC. With each side trying their hardest to be the ones to actually shoot themselves in the foot, and with the NBC business-affairs team finally managing to do just that.

The original deal for *Family Ties* was for four years. After that, NBC no longer controlled the rights to the show, and—theoretically, at least—Paramount could take the show to another network for years five, six, and beyond.

At the end of the second year, Paramount, responding to the slight uptick in *Family Ties* ratings, offered to sell NBC the rights to years five, six, and seven for a very modest increase in the license fee. Basically, they were willing to let it go for an extra five thousand dollars an episode and a gift certificate to the Wiz.

Luckily for me, the NBC guys flat-out refused to even discuss any restructure of the original deal. And then, everyone kind of forgot about it. And so, after year four, with *Family Ties* the number-two show on television, averaging about a 45 share, it was a rude surprise to NBC that they didn't own it anymore. And Christmas came early to Paramount and UBU that year.

Basically, each year *Family Ties* is on the air, NBC is required to put on another UBU show that year, as well. If we hit certain ratings or reach a certain number of episodes, this triggers other commitments. Everything I do seems to trigger another commitment, another show being produced. It's like, if I arrive at Paramount and park safely in my spot, it triggers another pilot being shot.

When you possess all these "commitments," it becomes a lot easier to interest people in your projects. And I'm getting to work with some extraordinary talent. We have a show on NBC now, *Sara,* created by Ruth Bennett, starring Geena Davis. Geena is a gifted actress and comedienne. Really smart, and a total pleasure to be around. I want to tell her, I wish you knew me before all this "success." I was a lot better.

Also in this cast, the brilliant Alfre Woodard, reveling in the opportunity to display her rich comic talent. Also, Bronson Pinchot. And this series also marks the network acting debut of a young, edgy, very funny comic, Bill Maher.

We're canceled after half a season.

We do a pilot, "Knights of the Kitchen Table," written by Bruce Helford, which follows a group of friends back and forth in time from childhood to adulthood. As the lead, I want to cast a young actor I admire and respect, George Clooney. George is, in *my* mind, a big star waiting to happen. He's a great guy. Funny, smart, engaging, and most important, a very good basketball player.

When I offer George the part, he tries to talk me out of giving it to him.

"Gary, you don't want to bring me in on this," he says. "I'm the kiss of death. I've failed in eleven pilots."

"You're the guy, George. Don't want anybody else."

"Don't do this to yourself. Bruce has written a great script. I'm only going to kill it."

Bruce and I both agree we love George and go ahead and hire him anyway. The pilot doesn't sell, keeping George's winless streak alive.

When George won the Oscar for his brilliant work in *Syriana,* I wrote him a note congratulating him. And I told him I thought it might be the right time now to go back to NBC and ask them to take another look at "Knights."

We have a show, *American Dreamer,* created by Susan Seeger, starring Robert Urich, who turns out to be a very talented, light-comic actor. It also features Jeffrey Tambor and Carol Kane, with recurring appearances by John Glover and Christine Ebersole. Canceled after one year.

We have a show starring a *Saturday Night Live* alum, Julia Louis-Dreyfus. Originally, Julia was the fourth lead in the show, *Day by Day,* created by Andy Borowitz and very loosely based on the Organic Day Care Center. But Julia quickly becomes our go-to guy. Clearly, even then, one of our most gifted actresses, Julia is incapable of being in a scene and not being funny. We're canceled after two seasons.

But I get an added bonus from my relationship with Julia. One night, at a dinner at Sam Weisman's house, I meet her husband, Brad Hall. This is our first meeting. He's so smart. And so funny. And so nice. Even though I've never read a word he's written, I ask him if he wants to come over to UBU, and he agrees. Brad and I will, in fact, do several TV shows together and two feature films.* And along with Sam, we'll collaborate on the creation of *Brooklyn Bridge,* one of the most satisfying experiences of my career. And Brad, a minister's son from Santa Barbara, will somehow channel 1950s Jewish people from Brooklyn, and author some of our very best scripts.

The idea to do the show began in 1991 with a phone call from Jeff Sagansky. Jeff had recently been named head of programming at CBS, and he was asking if I wanted to come over to do something for them. Anything. CBS was the number-three network at that time. And that's only because there were just three networks. Had there been a fourth, CBS would have been number four. But I liked and respected Jeff from our time together at NBC. And we agreed to go to lunch and talk about it.

At lunch I remember Jeff saying, "C'mon, there must be one thing you're dying to do. Let's do that." And I said there was one "thing" I had been thinking about. An area. A moment in time—1950s

American Dreamer, Brooklyn Bridge, Bye-Bye Love, Must Love Dogs.

Brooklyn. Stories centered around my neighborhood and my family. I even had a title ready for him: *My Grandmother's House.*

Jeff said he liked the idea of a 1950s comedy. Liked the idea of it being set in Brooklyn. And he thought *My Grandmother's House* was the worst title for a TV show he'd ever heard. I told him I'd try to think of another.

I came over to see Jeff at CBS the next week with a new title, *Brooklyn Bridge*, which he loved. I also had prepared several story ideas. Sketched out all the major characters. And pretty much took him through what the first season of this show would be like. He gave me a commitment on the spot to do thirteen episodes. And I set out to cast my family for TV.

Fortunately for me, Judith Weiner is back at my side as casting director. And on one glorious afternoon in New York, she brings in Peter Friedman, Louis Zorich, Danny Gerard, Matthew Louis Siegel, and Adam LaVorgna. Half the family right there. We find Amy Aquino in Los Angeles and now we have only one role left to cast. But it's the big one—Grandma Jenny.

I had originally written the part with Olympia Dukakis in mind. We had worked together on a feature film I directed, *Dad,** and, like anyone who's ever worked with Olympia, I fell madly in love. But she wasn't ready to commit to a TV series in Los Angeles at that point. And now we were having quite a lot of difficulty finding the right actress.

One day we received a call that Marion Ross wanted to come in and read for the part. I was skeptical, as was Judith. We loved Marion, and had great respect for her work in TV, films, and on stage. But in my mind, at least, she would always be Mrs. Cunningham, the quintessential Midwestern mom. Heir to the tradition of Jane Wyatt and Donna Reed. From places like Wisconsin and Minnesota, not Poland and Romania.

---

*Amblin-Universal, 1989. Starring Jack Lemmon, Ted Danson, Olympia Dukakis, Kathy Baker, Ethan Hawke, and Kevin Spacey.

Marion came in to read and was, in a word, marvelous. Charming and sweet and funny. Strong yet not overbearing. Just great. After she left the room I turned to Judith.

"Boy, she was great, huh?"

"Yeah. Absolutely."

"Too bad we know it's not going to be Marion Ross, eh?"

"Yeah, sad."

We see a lot of other actresses. All good. None right. Marion calls again. She'd like to come back in. She comes in a second time and, she's even better than she was the first time. After Marion left, I turned to Judith.

"Wow. She was even better than before."

"I know. That was perfect."

"She really made me laugh."

"Yeah."

"Too bad we know it's not going to be Marion Ross, huh?"

"It is too bad. Really. Because she's great."

We see still more actresses, none quite right, and then, one day, I turn to Judith.

"You know, maybe it *is* Marion Ross."

Marion will win the Golden Globe Award that first year for Best Actress in a Comedy Series. The show will also win a Golden Globe for Best Comedy. Two Viewers for Quality Television Awards for Best Comedy Series. Two more for Marion as Best Actress. A Humanitas Prize. A Christopher. Twelve Emmy nominations.

And then, be taken off the air after thirty-five episodes.

Some people have suggested the show didn't "work" because it was "too Jewish" and didn't play well outside New York and Los Angeles. But that simply wasn't true. Some of our strongest support was in the Midwest, South, and Southwest. My favorite letters would be from farm families in Montana or New Mexico, saying how my grandma was like their grandma—Grandma McClintock, or Grandma Rodriquez.

Truth is, we came up against three hard, immovable realities.

First, CBS, under Jeff's guidance, had soared into first place in the ratings race. And as much as they respected and were proud of our show, it was becoming a luxury they didn't want to afford. Second, the show was extremely expensive for Paramount to produce. And they didn't see a syndication rainbow over the horizon. So they were unwilling to pressure CBS to keep the show on. Third, the whole network television business was changing, beginning to focus primarily on attracting a specific group of viewers, rather than simply viewers. They wanted people eighteen to thirty-four, and our core viewing group was somewhat older.

Jeff Sagansky vividly illustrated this point to me one day. He had been besieged by calls from angry viewers berating him for not sticking with the show—for constantly changing time periods, and abruptly taking us off the air one day and then putting us back on the next, without much publicity, making the show difficult to locate. To his credit, Jeff tried to answer all these letters himself. Occasionally he even called people at home, trying to explain the CBS rationale.

One woman exemplified our problem. She was going in for open-heart surgery and she wanted to know if *Brooklyn Bridge* was coming back on the air. Because that would give her a reason to live. "So there you have it," Jeff said. "Your audience is extremely loyal. But they go in for a lot of surgery."

We were all crushed when we were taken off the air. The show had been an absolute joy to do. And we were all so proud of what we had accomplished. I did my best to try and console people and put it in some perspective for them.

"You know, you guys just lost a job in television. I had my childhood canceled."

But this bittersweet adventure is still four years in the future. Immersed in the UBU Empire at the moment, with multiple shows on the air, our weekdays are full. On the weekends we go out to a beach house we have in the northern end of Malibu, past Zuma Beach. What we like to think of as the more intellectual part of

Malibu. But Sylvester Stallone and Charo live on the same beach, so perhaps we're kidding ourselves.

This is the house that *Grease II* bought. In 1979, Paramount called me and said they were doing a sequel to *Grease* and they wanted me to write it. It was going to star Andy Gibb. I would have six weeks to write a draft. I would be well compensated. And there would be no time for a second draft.

I thought I was an odd choice to write *Grease II,* since I hadn't seen *Grease.* But, the Paramount people said no, I was the guy. They had a production date in place that fit in with a window on the Bee Gees' schedule, and they wanted someone who could write quickly. So they were looking to TV people to help them out.

I rented *Grease,* the original, and loved it. I thought it was totally charming. I figured the Paramount people obviously knew what they were doing. I was sure they knew exactly what they were looking for. And could provide me with a road map.

We met in New York. A lot of people with English accents, representing the Stigwood company. Pat Birch, the director, whom I liked immediately. And a couple of manager types representing Andy Gibb. The meeting itself had kind of a disco feeling, and I couldn't stop humming "Stayin' Alive" in my head.

After the usual small talk, one of the English guys turned to me and said, "What do you want to do?"

"What do *I* want to do?" I replied, my voice inexplicably several octaves higher, in a mini-homage to the Bee Gees, I guess. "I want to do what you want me to do."

"Don't you have an idea?"

"No. Don't you?"

This was not an auspicious start.

What they had was, indeed, minimal. Andy Gibb would play a cousin of Olivia Newton-John who was transferring to Rydell High. There was some notion of mistaken identity and something involving a motorcycle. That was it. And no one seemed overly worried about it.

I went off and wrote a script that I would generously describe as "functional." But I did only have six weeks, and everyone at Stigwood seemed surprisingly pleased with it. It was hard to tell. With their perfect English accents, everything they said, even the negative stuff, sounded encouraging. The movie was going forward.

One little wrinkle: It seems no one had ever actually seen Andy Gibb act. At the last minute, it was decided that there should at least be a screen test of sorts, so they could see what Andy's capable of. And also make whatever script adjustments needed to be made.

The "test" is set up at the Mill on the Paramount lot. I wander over to say hi to Andy, who couldn't be nicer or more polite. Just a sweet, almost shy, young guy. But it becomes immediately apparent that he's just not comfortable in front of the camera. All that charisma he possesses onstage has disappeared, and he's awkward and stilted. A lot like me in *Yum Yum Tree.*

The Paramount brass views the screen test and shuts the project down. Eventually, a few years later, *Grease II* does get made, starring Michelle Pfeiffer. I'm sent a copy of the script to see if I want to arbitrate and fight to get shared screenplay credit.

I have no grounds for arbitration. All that's left from my original script is half of one scene involving a motorcycle helmet and a jump.

And now this beach house.

The beach community is small, maybe forty homes, and reminds me a lot of the old neighborhood in Brooklyn. People drop in all the time without knocking. Kids come by and call Shana's name to come out and play. I sit out on the beach, my stoop, and kibbitz with people passing by.

We have a lot of friends who live on the same beach now. That's a big plus. Steven Spielberg lives nearby. Over the course of our now ten-year friendship, he's become a much-loved member of our extended family.

Diana and I have watched Steven gracefully deflect the perils of his success, approaching his work and his life with thoughtfulness and compassion. And a generosity of spirit that we admire and enjoy being around.

We look forward to seeing him on Saturday nights. And we're disappointed when he doesn't drop in. After dinner, a spirited game of rummy tiles or Trivial Pursuit. Baths for the kids. Herbal teas all around, and we're usually asleep by ten. Life in the fast lane.

It was in the living room of this little beach house that I tried to talk Steven out of the idea of doing *E.T.* He had sketched out the movie's main theme for us and then gone upstairs to make a phone call. When he was out of the room, I told Diana that I wanted to try and talk him out of making that movie.

"Why?" she asked. "It sounds like fun."

"It can't work," I told her, knowingly. "Look, Steven's become so big now, so successful, I think it's hard for people to tell him the truth anymore. As his friend, I think it's really important that I be honest with him."

"Well, I think it's a great idea for a film," she said. "And I don't remember him asking your opinion."

"Friends don't wait to be asked," I replied pompously.

When Steven came back into the room, I offered my sage advice. Always one to have my finger on the pulse of America, I explained to him that the time for this idea had passed. And I felt certain what was needed from him now was to turn his light to other, deeper, but still obviously commercial, subjects. Maybe something about Vietnam? Or the House Un-American Activities Committee? A musical biography of Eugene Debs?

Thank God he didn't listen! I'd hate to think I had anything to do with depriving the world of the pleasure of *E.T.*! And the fact that our friendship survived is a credit to Steven's willingness to overlook glaring "behavioral problems" in his friends.

One night Steven calls and asks if he can bring a friend over with him. One of his single buddies with nothing to do on a Saturday night. Diana and I are in our Saturday-night outfits of sweatpants and T-shirts when Steven arrives with his lonesome friend, who turns out to be Warren Beatty. Diana turns several colors not actually known to nature. And it looks like a sunset is breaking out on her forehead. She crosses quickly by me and starts up the stairs.

"Where're you going?" I ask her.

"Don't you know who that is?"

"Yeah."

"Well, I'm going upstairs to change! And put on makeup! And then I'm going to call my mother!!"

Mike will win the second of his three Emmys this year, for Best Actor in a Comedy Series. I will win this year, as well, for Best Comedy Script for "A, My Name Is Alex," which I co-wrote with Alan Uger.

The original script, which we read on Monday, was the standard half-hour length. But after the run-through on Tuesday, it became clear that this really wanted to be a one-hour episode. I called Brandon at home, to see if this was even possible. Brandon liked the idea and said, "Sure, go ahead." Then I told him I thought the second half of the show, where Alex visits a psychiatrist, the disembodied voice of actor David Wohl, and speaks directly to the camera, should be shown without the normal commercial interruption, which I felt would destroy the effect. There was a momentary hesitation, then, "Sure go ahead."

With Marc Lawrence making major contributions to the half-hour version of the script Alan Uger and I had written, we add about thirty-five pages to the script that night and turn it into a one-hour show. In the morning when I come onstage, Mike comes running over to me at a hundred miles an hour, and jumps on me.

"I'm going to kill with this. I got it. Thank you. I love it. I got it. I love you. Thank you."

In a way, that evening marked the high-water mark, at least for me, creatively. Mike would go on to win another Emmy in '88 and the Golden Globe in '89. He just continued to grow and dig deeper and work harder. But that old "creative tension" brought on by familiarity and success was getting harder and harder for me to shake entirely.

In the seventh year of *Family Ties,* around episode 165 or so, Mike, as Alex, was in an argument with Mallory about when she was going to get off the phone. He turned to me and laughed.

"Hey, Gar. Surely I've worked this out by now."

And it seemed like maybe it was time for us to go.

The final episode was almost impossible to get through. Several times we had to start over because one of the actors would begin crying. Makeup running, tears streaming, they would go off backstage to be "put together" again. Only to return to see this happen to another actor. And then another. And when Sam Weisman, the director, started crying, we knew we were going to be in for a long night.

We left quite a lot of money on the table by not coming back to do an eighth season. It was tempting. But in the end, it seemed like we had said all we wanted to say. Taken those characters as far as they could go within the confines of that family setting. We didn't want to abuse our relationship to those characters. Or abuse our relationship to the audience. And so on May 14, 1989, after 180 episodes, 90 hours, seven years, we went off the air. And we went off that week as the number-one show on television.

I was having lunch with Mike one day about seventeen years later, when he suddenly looked up from his chicken Caesar salad.

"We should've done the eighth year, huh?"

"Yeah."

1977

{chapter eighteen}

*H*ugh Wilson and I are writing and producing *The Tony Randall Show,* and the ratings are not good. We follow *The Jeffersons,* and I defy the network guys to show me the DNA of any individual who might want to sit down and watch both shows. Because I don't think such a person exists. But the handwriting is on the wall: We're going to be canceled.

Tony has been stalwart throughout all this, and unwavering in his support.

"I love the material, boys," he tells us. "I wish more people were watching. But I'm very proud of what we're doing."

When Hugh and I were first named producers, we went to Tony and laid our meager cards out on the table.

"Look, Tony, we have no business being the producers of this show," we began, figuring he probably already knew that. "But we are. And if you want to cut our balls off, there's nothing that we can do about it," figuring he knew that, too. "But if you do that, you'll have eunuchs for producers."

That was the risky part. What if he wanted eunuchs for producers? A lot of actors do. We were banking that Tony was too smart and too professional.

"If you let us produce the show we'll kill ourselves for you. We'll be available twenty-four hours a day, seven days a week. And we promise you'll be a full partner in all creative decisions."

Tony's eyes actually welled up with tears. "Boys, we're in this together. I promise."

He hugged Hugh. He hugged me. And then he made us all group-hug, at which point Hugh and I began to rethink the wisdom of our offer.

Always mercurial. Eccentric. Extremely talented. Underneath all the bluster, almost unbelievably sweet, Tony would live up to his promise. Onstage, in public, it was always, "What do the boys want?" Back in Hugh's office the arguments were more heated, and "what the boys want" was not always the guiding principle.

One time we were arguing about a particular line that Tony wanted out, when I suddenly realized that it wasn't even Tony's line. It was Barney Martin's. I pointed that out to Tony, but he stood firm.

"I won't be onstage with that line."

I burst out laughing. I couldn't help myself. Then Tony started laughing. Then Hugh. Then Tony hugged me. Then he hugged Hugh. Then he made us all group-hug. And Hugh and I again rethought the whole move-up-to-producer thing.

One time after rehearsal, we were discussing a scene that Hugh and I thought had actually gone quite well. Tony wanted it out and a new scene written in its place.

"But Tony," Hugh told him. "That scene completely worked."

"I can make anything work, boys. That's not the point. The point is, we can do better."

And most of the time, he was right.

The show was filmed on Tuesday night, and so the last rewrite Hugh and I would do would be on Friday night. We would always try to find the time to do one final pass for Tony. One last chance to make it better. To pay him back for all the trust he'd put in us. So he would know, for better or for worse, whatever the limitations of our talent, he had gotten everything we had to offer that week.

Saturday morning the phone would ring in my house. Tony calling with his reaction to the script. I could hear opera playing in the background. And Tony would go one of two ways.

"Boys, you did it."

Or, "Boys, I'll save you."

And he always said thank you.

My daughter Shana was attending kindergarten then, at the Oakwood School, near the MTM lot. Once in a while after school one of the gofers would pick her up and bring her to the set so I could see her. Later we could drive home together. When Shana would arrive on the set, Tony would stop the rehearsal and bring her over for a hug. Then he would get one of the big director chairs and put her up there right in the middle, facing the stage. He'd give her a pen and copy of the script.

"Now anything you see that you want changed just make a big X." He turned to me. "She's gotta know more than those guys at CBS."

Eventually, we were officially canceled, but Tony still refused to scapegoat me and Hugh. At the final wrap party he was sad but unbowed. He liked the work, and that was really all that mattered. At the end of the night we were together having a final drink.

"I only have one regret," he told me.

"What's that, Tony."

He looked at me a moment, then put a hand on my shoulder, "I wish I could buy stock in your future."

Tony and I stayed in touch over the years. Whenever I was in New York, we'd have breakfast at the Plaza. He kept up on my career. Was proud of the success of *Family Ties.* Couldn't get enough of Michael Fox, who he thought was brilliant.

"Reminds you of a young me, doesn't he?" he smiled.

I hadn't seen Tony for about five years at this point, but one night in 1997, when he was appearing on Broadway with Jack Klugman in *Sunshine Boys,* I went backstage after the show to surprise him. It was an old theater with a round wrought-iron staircase heading up to Tony's dressing room. I was with a friend of mine, David, from the old neighborhood. Tony came out on the balcony, struck a pose, and in a tone worthy of Macbeth:

"Goldberg, is that you?" Then, without missing a beat, "How's Diana? How's Shana?" He hugged me. Then he hugged David. Then he made us all group-hug. And this time, I was the one who didn't want to let go.

When he started his theater he called me for a contribution. "All right, let's face it. You owe me everything. You can deny me nothing. I have you down for *x* dollars."

"Check's in the mail, Tony." I hung up thinking, *I'm glad he didn't ask for 2x.* Because he was right. I could deny him nothing.

I was beginning to get some attention around town now, and there were a lot of different job offers coming my way. One day Jim Preminger came by to see me.

"I think you need to get a new agent."

"Why? What's the matter?"

"I can't keep pace with the offers that are coming in. I'm reading up on them the night before the meetings. I'm afraid I won't be able to represent you properly, that's all."

I told Jim, no way. He was my agent when no one else knew I was even in show business. He always believed in me, and I couldn't imagine anyone else representing me. Jim was happy to hear that. And he had an idea that might work for both of us. He wanted to bring into our "family" an attorney, Skip Brittenham, a real rising star in the world of entertainment law. That way, Jim could stay my agent and creative counselor, while Skip's business expertise and experience would allow Jim to feel that my interests were being properly protected.

Skip Brittenham absolutely rerouted the flow of money in Hollywood. And for the lucky few of us whom he represented then, his impact was akin to the impact Marvin Miller had on the salaries of athletes in professional sports.

My deal at MTM, as an example, which was typical of the way deals were being structured at that time, allowed for me to receive 12½ percent of the "net" profits of any show I created. The only problem being, there is no such thing as "net" profits. And there never will be. They don't exist. *Family Ties* has grossed close to a billion dollars worldwide, and I can give you today 100 percent of the "net" profits, and you can't buy a latte with it.

Skip thought we were in a "window in time" where we could change all that. The big studios were just now realizing that they had missed the boat on the potential riches to be gleaned from half-hour comedies. They had left that world (and all that money) to the Grant Tinkers, the Norman Lears. A small group of brilliant, creative businessmen. And, the studios now wanted to basically buy their way into that world.

It was similar to the flood of money being offered to baseball players in the newly created world of free agency. I remember, at the time, Cleon Jones of the Mets was being offered a million dollars to switch teams. Jones was a more than adequate ballplayer, but it was mind-boggling to think of him as a million-dollar player, when the great Mickey Mantle barely cracked $100,000, during his Hall of Fame career.

But Jones was at a lucky moment in time, when the rules were being rewritten. And so was I. I didn't want to leave MTM. I loved Grant Tinker and everything he represented. And I explained to Grant that I was being offered all this money even though I didn't actually deserve it. That I was kind of the Cleon Jones of writers. I remember Grant graciously making it easy for me.

"This is not a softball team," he told me. "You have a family. If you can get this money, take it. With my blessing."

Skip had one other radical new concept he wanted to introduce: Instead of just going around town to different studios and seeing what they were willing to offer, he was going to construct the whole deal himself—every element handcrafted and then submitted to the studios for them to consider. We were also going to go out with the deal to several studios at the same time. And in an effort to leverage our position and to see who was most interested, who was willing to "step-up," as Skip put it, he also set a time limit for their response.

"Can we at least read it?" one studio head joked.

"You can read it," Skip told him. "But you can't change it."

The deal Skip so brilliantly constructed provided for me to get 33⅓ percent of the "gross" of any show I created, a nice step up from my previous 12½ percent net. All the studios were interested in making the deal, which also included pay-or-play movie scripts, use of my own company logo, and a fund for me to develop projects independently. In the end, I chose Paramount to be my partner, really because of Gary Nardino.

Coming from MTM, where Grant was so proactively supportive of the creative process, I was wary of studio interference. And I was nervous I'd get swallowed up in the big studio culture. When I met with Nardino, I told him about the freedom I wanted. How I felt it was the best way for me to work. And ultimately would result in the best shows for us.

I told him about the first run-through we had on *The Tony Randall Show,* after Hugh and I had taken over as producers. We were waiting for Grant Tinker to arrive, and were almost a half hour behind schedule, when we decided to call and see what was happening. Grant seemed surprised. He said if we really wanted him to come, he would, but he wasn't sure that it was necessary.

"You're going to be there, right? And Hugh is there?"

"Yeah."

"Well, tell me how it went. And let me know if there's anything I can do to help."

"OK."

"And Gary, it's your show, not mine. Never hold a run-through for me."

Nardino twitched involuntarily.

This was obviously not standard operating procedure at Paramount.

"If you try to screw around with me," I told him. "I won't fight you. But you'll have a very expensive guy writing novels on Paramount stationery."

Nardino weighed my words. What life together might be like. He was a tough guy from New Jersey. Very smart.

"All right," he said. "I've got other guys I can screw around with."

And I knew right there I had my partner. He didn't deny that he did things like that. He just said he wasn't going to do it with me. And he never did.

Paramount was still a huge cultural shift for me. It was like going from a small college like Amherst and transferring to Michigan State. I realized how sheltered I was at MTM. How protected. I also saw for the first time that not all writers worked only on projects that they passionately believed in. Some were simply writers for hire. A category that didn't exist at MTM.

I remember meeting one of the writers on a new Paramount series, *Here's Boomer*.

"Oh, right," I said. "That's the show that has the talking dog."

"The dog doesn't talk," the guy shot back, angrily. "You hear his thoughts. It's a totally different thing."

"Oh."

"I wouldn't work on a show with a talking dog."

"Gotcha."

Here's Boomer was the highest-testing show in the history of TV up to that point, by the way. And was canceled within six weeks. Some of the lowest-testing shows of all time: *Seinfeld*, *The Mary Tyler Moore Show*, *All in the Family*. Perhaps there's a lesson here, I don't know.

Paramount was to be my home for twelve years. They offered nothing but support and encouragement the whole time. And we enjoyed great success together.

When *Family Ties* was being sold into syndication in 1985, we were all standing around in Nardino's office waiting for the responses from the various local stations across the country. I was with Greg Meidel, one of Paramount's senior business gurus and a guy I really came to like and respect. The whole selling process had been an eye-opener for me. These guys were every bit as creative and inventive as any of the guys working on the shows they were syndicating.

After an agonizing wait, the first bid comes in. New York.

"This is good, Gary," Greg Meidel said, studying the numbers. "This is very good."

Diana and I were hoping at that time to move up to a house in the Brentwood area. With two kids now, we were hoping for a little more room and a little larger yard. And we had a particular house in mind that we had seen and liked.

Then the next two bids come in. Chicago and Los Angeles. Greg whistles softly.

"I don't believe this!"

"Is it good, Greg?"

"It's a lot more than good."

"So, can I buy a house in Brentwood?"

Greg Meidel laughed. "Gary, you can buy Brentwood."

1990

{ chapter nineteen }

*D*iana and I have been together twenty-one years now. We have two daughters, Shana, soon to be eighteen, and Cailin, coming up on seven. And we're thinking it might be time for us to get married. Our relationship, our commitment to each other, has always been very personal and very private. A compact, just between the two of us. But it feels like it may be the right time now to acknowledge to the community at large that we think the relationship is working.

If you've found real love, just as if you've found real religion, you're a blessed individual. And it's best, I believe, to live those values quietly. Because so much of it, sometimes, in relationships, is just plain timing and luck. There were times when I was ready to give up on us as a couple. And there were times when Diana was ready to give up. But fortunately we were never both ready to give up at the same time. And so, after whatever terrible fight we had, whatever harsh words had been spoken, whichever one of us was stuffing clothes into a backpack and trying to figure out whose books and records were whose, the other one would come in and quietly say, "No. Not yet. Not now. Let's give it one more try."

In an odd way, I think the fact that we weren't legally married made us less willing to have our relationship torn asunder. At first, it was a point of rebellious pride. "We don't need no piece of paper from the city hall"* to validate our behavior. And it was romantic and empowering to think that each day we were, in effect, deciding to stay together. Then it became a part of our identity. The face we showed the world, as a couple. And it was exciting to try and define exactly who we were to each other with no preconceived notions about the meaning of *husband* and *wife*.

When we went in together to open our first joint bank account, the young female clerk asked us what our relationship was. Diana said, "Friends." At that exact same moment, I said, "Lovers." I think between the two of us, we got it right.

When Diana and I first met, in 1969, although we couldn't have articulated it, on some level we both wanted to change who we were and alter the course of where we were going. And somehow we were each able to see in the other a picture of the very best self that other person could become.

Up to this point, Diana had spent a great deal of her life making other people happy. As the oldest daughter in a conservative Catholic family, she had responsibilities and she had chores. There was a right way to do things. There were rules. And there were boundaries. There was propriety. There was decorum. And she was trying to gather the courage to push harder against those fences and forces trying to corral her. And from the first moment I saw Diana, I could only picture her running free.

As for me, I could have used some boundaries. If you knew me fifteen minutes, you knew my whole life story. After eighteen minutes, you were invited to move in. There was no propriety, precious little decorum, and certainly no rules. It was as if I was part of an Indian tribe that had no word for "tomorrow."

At the same time, I was trying to free myself from what had become a narrow and confining macho sports culture. I wanted to expand the Brooklyn world view, which was about winning at all costs, and learn to enjoy simply playing and competing. Letting

---

*Joni Mitchell, from "My Old Man," on *Blue*, Reprise, June 1971.

the process itself be the pleasure, not the outcome. I wanted to believe I had a softer, more artistic side. And Diana looked at me as if I did. As if I actually had depth—Another concept for which my tribe had no word.

Growing up in New York there were no neutral encounters. Every event had a winner and a loser. Not only in sports, the obvious arena, but in shopping, in buying a car, in eating in restaurants. In junior high school once, we were playing an away game up in Connecticut, and on the bus trip north, we stopped for lunch outside a smorgasbord restaurant, which was "all you can eat." The coach told us to "huddle up" in the rear of the bus, and he explained to us what we had to do to "win" this.

"OK, listen up. When you walk in, you're going to see, right there at the front of the table, a lot of salad stuff. A lot of rolls, potatoes, vegetables. Don't touch any of that. That's what they want you to do. That stuff costs them nothin'. You fill your plate with that stuff, you lose. What you gotta do is pass that all by and go right to the meat. That's the big-ticket item here. That's how you win this, fellas. Listen to me, this is important. Eat the meat to beat the house."

Insanely, fifty years later, I remember that pep talk. And perhaps more insanely, I've given it to my own kids.

Being a waiter at the Village Gate was also quintessentially New York, and definitely a contact sport with winners and losers. As a customer, for example, if you ordered a brand-name Scotch, say Chivas, or Dewar's, or Johnnie Walker, you were charged an additional dollar.

I would go in the kitchen and order. One Dewar's. One Chivas. One Johnnie Walker. Mike, the surly bartender, would reach behind him for the bottle of "Herbie's" scotch, brewed around the corner on Thompson Street, and proceed to pour from that single bottle into my three different shot glasses, pointing out as he poured:

"This one's the Dewar's. This one's the Chivas. This is the Johnnie Walker."

"Which one's the Dewar's?"

"Fuck you."

Coming back out into the main room, and at the table now, I take one glass off the tray, and dramatically hold it up to the light.

"Who had the Chivas?"

On the flip side, customers routinely tried to run out on the check without paying. If this happened, you were screwed, because you then had to pay that whole check yourself, and you'd be working the rest of the night just to get back to zero.

Everyone at the Gate had a partner, so that the floor was never left unguarded. You'd take an order, go in, and fill it, while your partner stayed out to make sure no one bolted on you without paying. My regular partner at the Gate was James Collier. James was a tall, handsome, black kid from a small town in Mississippi, and one of the sweetest, kindest, gentlest men I ever met. To say James was bisexual would be to diminish the scope of what he was able to accomplish on any given evening. I used to enjoy watching him go over to a table to take orders and watch the women immediately sit up straighter and check their hair. Sometimes some of the guys would check their hair too, and I knew it was going to be a good night for us, as we split tips fifty-fifty.

One very snowy night, I see James in the kitchen having a Brandy Alexander, and I just have a bad feeling about what's going on out at our station. Sure enough, when I come back out into the main room I see it right away. Empty table. Check still sitting there. No cash on top. It had been a well-dressed, older man, slutty, model-hooker younger girl, couple. My favorite combination.

I grab the check and dash out the side door, heading out onto Bleecker Street. As I come out into the cold night air, I catch a glimpse of the two of them getting into a taxi heading south, and I take off, running as fast as I can, given the snowy conditions. Luckily, these same conditions keep the cab from gaining too much speed, and I catch up halfway down the block and start banging on the roof of the cab. When the cab stops, I open the back door and get in. The guy seems more amused than anything else. The girl seems frightened.

"You forgot to pay this," I tell him, holding up the check.

"You're kidding. I'm so sorry."

"You know, this money's important to me. I'm in college, and this is my tuition. I'm pre-med."

"This should make everything OK, then, I hope."

He hands me a hundred-dollar bill. I take it and start to crawl out of the cab.

"What kind of doctor are you going to be?"

I stop, look back over at the girl. "Gynecologist."

When I get back, James is still in the kitchen, having yet another Brandy Alexander. I show him the hundred-dollar bill. He smiles.

"Pre-med or pre-law?"

Diana and I aren't certain what kind of marriage ceremony we want to have. We're both wary of large public displays of affection and of drawing attention to ourselves. We feel that, way too often, the bigger the party, the smaller the actual commitment that's underneath. I remember being at a big-time Hollywood party where the happy husband had taken over all of Chasen's restaurant and then tented the parking lot outside, because the restaurant itself couldn't contain the depth of his love and affection for his wife of twenty happy years.

"To my wife for life." He raised his glass, and we all joyfully joined in.

Three weeks later they were separated, and it turns out he was having an affair with his secretary for at least ten of the past twenty happy years. Great party, though!

In the end, we decide we're just going to go down to City Hall and get married in a civil ceremony. We're not going to tell anyone, not even the kids. We drive down in separate cars, since I'm going to be going in to work after, and, of course, I go to the wrong city hall, thinking that we're getting married in Santa Monica, when, evidently, we're getting married in downtown L.A., which, evidently, Diana has explained to me more than one time, and, evidently, I have forgotten. We have one last argument before the ceremony, which we feel helps make it a more traditional wedding, anyway.

Inside the correct city hall now, downtown L.A., we're waiting with a lot of other people, almost none of whom speak English. There are large family groups, lots of kids of all ages, a lovely feeling of community and festivity, loud and lively. We help take pictures, fix dresses, bounce babies. The time passes quickly, and then a young guy, looking a lot like Freddie Prinze sipping a huge Coca-Cola from McDonald's, calls out our names in a thick Spanish accent. He's dressed in a T-shirt and jeans, and he motions for us to come through a wooden side door, and when we enter, we see him stepping into his robe, and after one last sip of his coke, he turns to us and asks if we're ready. Only then, do we realize he's the guy who's going to be marrying us.

As he puts aside his Coke and gathers up his Bible and zips up his robe, he is transformed, somehow, into a young man of enormous dignity and presence. There is a sparkle of divinity in his eyes as he asks us if we realize the seriousness of the union we're about to enter into. We nod and say we think we do have some idea. And in this little nondescript room, with "Freddie Prinze" looking over us, when we come to that part where we say, "I do," and we promise to "love and honor," both Diana and I have tears running down our cheeks, and when we look over at "Freddie," we notice he is crying just a little too.

In the morning, when I come down, Shana's studying at the breakfast table. I haven't seen her, yet, although Diana did get a chance last night, to tell the kids what happened. As I walk by, Shana barely glances up. Small smile on her lips.

"Oh, Pa," she says. "Congratulations on the nuptials."

1996

{chapter twenty}

I'm leaning out the window of our apartment on Central Park West, and I'm screaming out into the night, "I need some money! Send me some money, please! I need fourteen million dollars. Help!"

This money's not for me. It's for the Archer School. A girls' school Diana cofounded in Los Angeles, which, it turns out, I'm going to be funding.* I've been told by the psychic that the universe is poised to help this project, but I have to be very specific about what I need. I have to ask for the money out loud. And I have to say "please" and "thank you." Evidently, the universe is very big on politeness.

I lean out into the night one last time, and scream. "Please send me fourteen million dollars. That's one-four. Thank you." And then, as an afterthought, I add, "I love you," thinking, how can it hurt?

I'm wondering how many other people in the building might be leaning out their windows right now, asking the universe for money. Bono lives above me in the penthouse. What if he's asking for money? The universe seems to like him a lot! What if he gets my money? I make a note to audit Bono.

---

*The other cofounders were Megan Callaway and Vicky Shorr—two brave, stalwart women. I leave it to their own husbands to write books about them. And they should.

The Archer School was born three years ago, the first girls' school founded in California, since all the research that had come out that proved that girls actually do learn differently from boys. And this school will be designed from the ground up to take advantage of those differences.

The school began in the basement of a dance studio in Pacific Palisades, with thirty-three girls, one of whom was our younger daughter, Cailin, now fifteen. An immediate unqualified success, we now have two hundred fifty students, and we're in the process of trying to buy the Eastern Star Home on Sunset Boulevard, a beautiful old Spanish building with a sprawling seven-acre campus behind it, to accommodate our growing population.

What's complicating everything is that the move of the Archer School from the Palisades to Brentwood is being opposed by a group of mean-spirited neighbors who live near the Eastern Star and are spreading some vicious lies about the school, the girls, and the impact Archer will have on the Brentwood community. They've organized themselves into a group with the high-minded name "Concerned Citizens of Brentwood." And while some of the members might be genuinely concerned about the community, others are quietly concerned with buying the Eastern Star Building themselves, then tearing down that beautiful structure and putting up wall-to-wall condominiums.

They have a very slick campaign in place, and it seems to be working. There are "Say No to Archer" signs up and down Sunset Boulevard. Advertisements against us in the local paper. At an anti-Archer fundraiser, one of our nastiest opponents, a wealthy banker, loudly boasts that the Archer School will go into the Eastern Star Home over his "dead body." I want to tell him I know a couple of guys in my old neighborhood who can accommodate him.

Their big issue, the big bogeyman they're using, is traffic. It's a fake issue, because we've already filed an environmental impact report showing that moving the school into Eastern Star will actually help mitigate the traffic problem on Sunset Boulevard. For one thing, Diana and I have already spent 3 million dollars of our own money widening Sunset and putting in two left-turn lanes on Barrington, the adjacent street. We've also paid to synchronize all the traffic lights. We've agreed that all our kids will be bussed to school. And in a further effort to help relieve the congestion, we're willing to start classes forty-five minutes earlier than the other schools in the area.

We've been assured by the psychic that this is a battle we will eventually win, but it's really getting ugly out there. There's an added element of racism involved, I believe, because of the scholarship program, which is at the heart of the school's mission: "To Educate Girls—all kinds of girls from all kinds of backgrounds—in a community where the best teachers can do their best teaching based on the research about the way girls learn."

That's the really genius piece of the founders' dream. This will not simply be a school for rich kids. Archer will, by charter, maintain a 20–25-percent scholarship base and will have one of the most ethnically diverse school populations in California, if not the country. This doesn't sit well with some of the "Concerned Citizens," who have been making not-so-veiled remarks about girls coming to Archer from "out of the neighborhood."

Diana's on a crusade here to change the way young girls are educated. The Archer School will alter the lives of many of the girls who attend, particularly the lives of our scholarship students, primarily African-American and Latina girls from the South Side of L.A. We will place these girls at Princeton, at Brown, at Stanford, at Yale. It's a revolution. I'm living with Leon Trotsky.

When Diana and I do grasp exactly who we're up against and the shameful nature of their "crusade," it becomes clear to us that we cannot go on with our lives if these people are allowed to win. We pledge everything we have, mortgage our home, encumber our pension. We'll go back to living in a tent before we'll let these "concerned" citizens destroy the dream of the Archer School.

And that's how I come to find myself screaming out into Central Park in the middle of the night. I need fourteen million dollars to buy the Eastern Star building, and I've come to New York City to work on *Spin City,* a show I cocreated with a very talented young writer, Bill Lawrence. I've also come to be reunited with the other love of my adult life (after Diana), Michael J. Fox.

It's a complete fluke that Michael and I have been reunited. After *Family Ties* ended in 1989, we each went our separate way. We stayed in contact by phone and Christmas cards, occasionally we'd get together for a cup of coffee and a hug, but creatively, we were each busy pursuing different paths. I kept a proud eye on his soaring movie career. He kept up with my work in TV, even coming out to direct an episode of *Brooklyn Bridge* in 1991. But living on different coasts, and with families to raise, our time together was infrequent.

Then one day, around Christmas 1995, the phone rang, and it was Michael calling. We exchanged the usual holiday greetings and family news, and then he asked me if I thought he should sign a letter that was to appear in *Variety* in support of our former boss at Paramount, John Pike. John had been accused, unjustly I believed, of making insensitive remarks about certain ethnic groups and had, in fact, been forced to resign from his job at CBS, where he had been in charge of late-night programming. I told Mike I was going to sign it. I knew John, liked him a lot. He'd been a great partner for us at Paramount, and I couldn't imagine that he could be guilty of something like this. Mike said that was his instinct too, and he was definitely going to sign the letter.

We were saying our good-byes, when Mike told me he was coming back to TV, which was a big surprise. He was tired of all the travel that seems to come with making movies, tired of being away from his family, and he was going to do a show in New York with ABC. He said he hadn't asked me to get involved because he knew I wouldn't be interested in moving to New York. He was right about that part, but still I felt a momentary pang that Mike would be back on TV and I wouldn't be a part of it. I guess I was jealous that someone else would have that great pleasure of working with Mike, but I got over it quickly and wished him, very sincerely, all the best with his new project.

A few nights later, we're having dinner with Jeffrey Katzenberg, and I tell Jeffrey of my phone call from Mike. How happy I am for him. How excited he seems about going back to TV.

"It's not happening."

Jeffrey who knows everything, tells me.

"The script came in, and Mike didn't like it. He has script approval, and the project's dead."

I say I'm sorry it didn't work out for Mike. He certainly deserves material he's in love with, and luckily he's in a position where he can just wait for the right script to come his way. I then confess my little pang of jealously upon hearing of Mike's potential return to TV without me.

Jeffrey, who has a keen nose for what's not said and for any budding opportunity to do business, doesn't miss a beat.

"Would you want to work with Michael again?"

"Of course. Who wouldn't jump at the chance to work with Mike?"

I explain that one of the deal breakers for Mike, though, is to have the show film in New York City, and I don't see how I can do that. I turn to Diana, expecting her to agree, and, always one to surprise, she says, "That might be fun."

The next thing I know, I'm on the DreamWorks jet heading to New York to meet with Mike. Jeffrey has brokered this whole thing, as only he can. He told Mike I have a hundred ideas for him, which is not exactly true, since at this moment I don't have any. And he told me that Mike was dying to work with me again, which also wasn't exactly true. Mike was very concerned about us teaming up again. He is to be a full partner on this project, not just an actor for hire but also the co-executive producer. I think he was afraid I'd always see him as the young guy I "discovered," rather than the grown man he has become. Also, Mike, who is as fearless as he is talented, wanted to step out in a whole new creative direction, into an edgier, darker kind of comedy than we had done together before, and he had some serious questions about whether I was willing to go there myself, as a writer.

And that's why, seated across from me on this elegant Gulfstream aircraft, headphones on, hat turned backward, reading *Cosmopolitan* magazine, is twenty-seven-year-old Bill Lawrence. I had brought Bill over to UBU Productions in 1995, after he had gotten fired from *Friends*. I'm always interested in hiring writers who've been fired from other shows. It usually means one of three things: 1) The writer is untalented, which is rarely the case; 2) they couldn't shut up and sign off quietly on mediocre material; or 3) they have a personality whose quirks are intimately tied up with their talent but ultimately difficult to be around. And number three explains how two extremely talented and very nice people like Marta Kauffman and David Crane could let someone like Bill Lawrence go.

Bill has a hundred ideas every fifteen minutes, ninety-eight of which are useless; but two of them are brilliant and can come from no other person on the planet. He was story editor on a short-lived show we did on ABC the previous year, *Champs*, and I really came to respect his talent, his incredible work ethic, and his absolute inability to say, "This is good enough. Let's stop."

Bill would always pitch one more idea. Try one more different way to do the scene. Call you in the middle of the night with an idea he just had. This behavior can get you fired, true. But, it can also get you on a Gulfstream going to New York to write a pilot for Michael Fox.

Bill takes off his headphones and passes the *Cosmopolitan* over to me. He's circled his horoscope for January. Incredibly, it reads, "You are on a trip to fortune and fame. Great riches and success await you at your destination." Bill smiles and puts his headphones back on. I make a note to subscribe to *Cosmopolitan*.

The truth is, I share some of Michael's concerns myself. Not so much about working together again, but whether this kind of comedy we're contemplating is something I can do well. The old *Family Ties*, *Cheers*, style of comedy is now being challenged in some very exciting new ways. Our storytelling structure on *Family Ties* was relatively simple. Six scenes of seven pages or so, and a short tag. There was an "A" story and a "B" story. Sometimes they connected. More often they didn't. And in the last scene, Alex would apologize, and the two stories would resolve and end.

A show like *Friends,* in contrast, might have fifteen scenes, four story lines, very little if anything resolved at the end. Continuing "arcs" from week to week. It's an interesting storytelling style, and one I'm drawn to. It lets you do short scenes, just the heart—get a big joke and cue the music. It's energizing, and I'm eager to explore but still learning the rules of the road. And Bill is my guide to this new comedy world I want to embrace.

On the way over to the Four Seasons to meet Mike, I get my first lesson in the new behavior patterns. It's a blustery, cold New York day, and I have my overcoat buttoned to the top.

"Only old guys button their coats," Bill tells me.

"Really?"

"Absolutely."

He opens his coat. "Young," he says. Then, closing his coat, "Old." He repeats several times, opening and closing his coat. "Young." "Old." "Young." "Old."

I open my coat. I'm still old, and now I'm also cold. But evidently I look young.

On the flight to New York, we have come up with an area that we like for Mike. New York City politics. He will be the deputy mayor to a kind of befuddled, Reaganesque chief executive. This will allow him to, in effect, be the one making policy, and it gives him some strong comedy "through-lines"—a mayor to protect, news media to deflect, a big city to govern. When you have Mike Fox, you start with intelligence and a need to control. A connection to, but not a slavish devotion to, the truth. A guy walking right up to the line of unethical behavior, but not crossing it. Alex Keaton with power.

I had forgotten how much fun it is to be in a room with Mike. How smart he is. How funny. He and Bill hit it off immediately. We sketch out other characters, a hapless press secretary, a jealous colleague who wants Mike's job, a hard-nosed female reporter with whom Mike's having an affair.

Mike is getting really excited now. He wants to do a show that people will talk about the next morning. A show where people will say, "I can't believe they did that." And professionally, he wants to prove himself to a whole new generation of TV viewers. No resting on his laurels, nothing that he's done before. No free ride.

With hugs from Mike, Bill and I go off to write. We write the *Spin City* pilot in four days. It's so great having Mike's voice in my head again. Bill's proving to be the perfect writing partner. We fax Mike the script, and fifteen minutes later we get a fax back from him. "I love it. I'm in. Let's make a show."

1997

*I*t's 2:30 in the morning, and I'm sitting in my apartment in New York, looking out over Central Park. The lamplights twinkle below, their reflections, shimmeringly beautiful, bounce off the Bow Bridge. Nina Simone plays on the CD—her live album, *Nina at the Village Gate.* If I listen carefully, I can almost hear myself spilling drinks in the background. My feet are up, my head tilted back, I'm sipping from a glass of very expensive, very delicious red wine. And I am as unhappy as I've ever been in my entire life.

Michael Fox and I have radically different ideas about the direction of the new show we're doing, *Spin City*. Radically different ideas about the main character, Mike Flaherty. And we disagree about almost every other element of the show, as well. From the costumes to the music to the warm-up guy. In the best-case scenario for Mike, I would be replaced. My best-case scenario is that I had never agreed to do this in the first place.

In Mike's eyes, when he looks at me, I see disappointment, resentment, frustration. In mine he can see the same.

Bill Lawrence is the go-between for me and Mike. Doing shuttle diplomacy between the two of us, like they do in the Middle East. With similar results.

"Boss, you gotta smile a little more, you know. It's kind of obvious you're not happy."

"I'm a terrible actor, Bill. I've got the reviews to prove it."

The pilot episode, which Bill and I wrote, and Tommy Schlamme directed, was very well received. The ratings put us in the top five and the reviews were uniformly excellent. It seemed that we had pulled off something very difficult here. To make people "forget" Alex P. Keaton and Marty McFly, Mike's two cultural icon characters, and make room for a third version of Mike Fox for people to fall in love with, in the person of Michael Flaherty. And it was a tribute to Mike's enormous talent that it was succeeding. I remember how proud I felt when he told me one day that someone had passed him on the street and just said "Yo, Mike Flaherty. Way to go."

But it was downhill for us from then on. Early in the season, Mike was a guest on *Letterman,* and all the writers gathered in the conference room to watch him. Mike's one of the few actors I know who really doesn't need anyone to write material for him for these interviews. In truth, in those situations, no writer could capture Mike's warmth, his playfulness, his intelligence, his ability to be funny out there on his own.

Mike was being his charming and engaging self when Letterman asked him what kind of character he played on *Spin City* and Mike said, "Well, I play this kind of weasel." At that point I jumped up and started screaming at the screen, "No, no, Mike Flaherty's not a weasel. Mike Fox is not a weasel. He's the antiweasel."

After Bill Lawrence wrestled me back into my chair and the other writers applied cold compresses and I was offered and served warm herbal tea and my feet were elevated and my blood-pressure checked, 1500 over 750, which I think is normal, I called Mike at home.

"Hey."

"Hey."

"Great show, Mike."

"Thanks, love Letterman."

"He loves you."

"They loved the clip I showed. Studio audience really laughed. I don't know if you could tell."

"Mike, you're not a weasel."

"Huh?"

Our primary role model for the character of Mike Flaherty was George Stephanopoulos. Choir-boy cute and movie-star handsome at the same time, fiercely intelligent, and possessing a clear and strong code of ethics and behavior, George was also a guy who knew how to win. And was willing to do whatever was necessary to achieve his aims. But he wasn't a weasel. Ever.

George was very generous with his time in helping us sketch out the Mike Flaherty character.* He told hilarious stories about the high-stakes world of backroom politics. And he was very candid about the complicated relationship that exists between a chief executive and his chief of staff.

"If I get up in the morning and it's raining," George told us, "my first thought is, how does this affect my guy? Yankees lost last night. How does this affect my guy? Everything that happens can affect my guy. Everything. And I have to make sure it affects him positively."

Mike Flaherty's character begins to come into focus for me and Bill. He is smart. He is charming, disarming, always focused on "his guy."

Our guiding principle becomes: "In a world where bad guys win, where people lie regularly and cheat routinely, our guy knowing all this and also from time to time employing these same tactics, every once in a while our leader, Michael Flaherty, will turn ever so slightly toward the light."

But Mike doesn't seem to want to turn toward the light. Not even a little. He only wants to be dark. He enjoys playing a guy who never explains. Who never apologizes. He's always asking,

---

*Kevin McCabe and Sid Davidoff also gave generously of their time and political expertise.

"Where's the weird?" And I feel deeply that America does not want to tune in each week to see Mike Fox be weird. To see him be dark. To see him uncaring and uninvolved. And I can't for the life of me figure out how to write that.

And so I'm sitting home alone feeling sorry for myself, having left work "early" at two A.M. so Bill and the writing staff can do the changes that Mike wants done. The writers routinely work all through the night, and many of them have taken to sleeping in the office. It's just easier.

I won't do any of the actual writing myself anymore. I'm not willing to offer my own work up into a universe where it can be arbitrarily and summarily rejected almost before it's even put on its feet. It's the exact opposite of how we worked on *Family Ties*. But this is how Mike wants it. Or more fairly, in my own confusion and frustration, this is how I perceive Mike wants it.

One great thing, though, about being back in New York is, I get to see all my old Brooklyn friends again. It's like being back in high school with money. On Thursday nights, we gather up at Carmine's on Ninetieth and Broadway. We eat and drink a lot. Debate the major philosophical issues of the day: Whether you play some defense man-to-man against an out-of-bounds play from underneath the other team's basket. Whether, when you're up three with time running out, you foul immediately. Or just play good D and guard against the three-point shot?*

We talk about that game we lost by one point in Madison Square Garden a mere thirty-four years ago now.

And, within fifteen minutes: "You didn't foul that guy, Fred."

"No way."

"Bad call."

"Fuck that ref."

There's a chorus of "Fuck that ref" now, and I join in. Sure, we're

---

*For the record, I believe you play zone out of bounds. And no foul, up three with time running out.

running out of time to get over this. But you know what? It *was* a bad call.

The guys come to see the show every Friday night. They sit in the front row, providing moral support and the basis for a very good laugh track. Early Saturday morning, we all go back to Lafayette to play full-court basketball together. Then it's out to Coney Island for a stop at Nathan's. Then I continue out to Kennedy and hop on the three P.M. American flight to Los Angeles. That night I have dinner in Malibu at Granita with Grant Tinker. The collision of my two worlds.

I'm really enjoying being around the staff of young writers we've assembled. We have fourteen altogether. And for twelve of the fourteen, this is their first job. They're smart and funny. Very sweet. And I'm impressed by their energy and enthusiasm. How hard they work. How much they care.

Sometimes, after work, we'll all go out as a group. Some very hip new club someone's discovered. Bad lighting. Lumpy couches. A couple of wool blankets. Very retro '50s, which I guess is the idea. It looks like Judy Berkowitz' basement, where we'd have our junior-high-school parties.

I'm on the phone with Diana, telling her how much I enjoy these evenings out with the writing staff.

"Even though I'm so much older," I explain, pridefully, "they really seem to like having me around."

There's a beat of silence, then Diana asks, "Who pays?"

When I think about it, the check does always seem to make its way over to me at the evening's end. I mention that to Bill Lawrence. He waves me off. "Coincidence," he says. "Pure random luck. Roll of the dice." In fact, they're all going to go out tonight. Very new hip place. Just opened. Impossible to get in. And all the writers want me to come along as their guest.

That night at the ultrahip new place, which is in some part of lower Manhattan barely tethered to the island, we gather to drink martinis and smoke cigars. The room is the very essence of '50s rumpus-room "elegance." It looks like a place you play spin the bottle. But the drinks are hefty, and I do love the company.

At the end of the evening I look down, and there in front of me, somehow magically, is the check. I look over at Bill.

He shrugs, "Sorry, boss. We tried."

Spin City, while very successful, is also very expensive, and we're getting some pressure from DreamWorks and Jeffrey Katzenberg about the costs. I try to explain some of the delays. It's a new show. Finding our way. New style of shooting, with five cameras. One day out on location for exteriors. Really, we're making a mini-movie each week.

Jeffrey asks about all the rewriting. The scripts thrown out. The days we shut down. I don't want to go too much into the problems between Mike and me, but Jeffrey's a smart guy, and he can read between the lines.

One day they send a young guy to New York, a business guy, who's going to keep an eye on us and find places to cut costs. I find this a little bit offensive, because it presupposes that we're not interested in keeping the costs down ourselves, and that's really not true. But anyway, this guy is here and he seems nice enough. At first.

I explain to him what I think his situation is.

"Did you see *Apocalypse Now?*" I ask him.

"Sure."

"Well, you're the Martin Sheen character. And they've sent you upriver to die."

"I don't think so."

"Neither did Martin Sheen."

I explain to him my belief that Katzenberg, who's great and a real friend to me and Mike, can't really come here himself, so he's sent this fella to snoop around, knowing that, if this guy pisses off me or Mike, Jeffrey can just fire him and then blame him for being overly aggressive. For "misunderstanding" the mission. This guy's only hope of remaining "alive," I explain to him, is for him to not get in our way.

He doesn't see it that way. And he's already come up with some ideas about how we can find immediate savings. First thing he'd like to do is cut back on the bagel allotment for the writers. We're about $250,000 a week over budget at this point, and I'm not confident we're going to find the savings we need in the bagel account, but hey, what do I know? I'm fifty-two. I've been doing this for twenty years. This guy's eleven, and I think this is his first show, but he seems very certain about his position. He would also like to see us cut back on cream cheese, if not eliminate it entirely.

And so begins one of the stupidest chapters of my life, dubbed by the young writers the Condiment Wars. If the people at Dream-Works want to see just how big a shmuck I can become, I am more than ready to show them.

The first thing I do is double the bagel order, adding blueberry and pineapple bagels, even though no one in New York would ever actually eat one of those, but that's not the point, and they do add some color to the breakfast basket. Then I up the ante by adding scallion cream cheese into the mix. A clear shot across the bow. And, I explain to the writing staff that everyone has to eat at least one bagel a day, and those who can step up to the challenge should eat two.

The plan is working well, at first, with everyone pitching in and doing their share. But then some of the young women start to complain.

"I'm having trouble fitting into my jeans," Amy Cohen whines.

"I have a wedding coming up at Christmas, and I bought a new dress I won't be able to wear"—from Michelle Nader.

I buy Amy some new jeans and offer to pay to have Michelle's dress let out. I drop them each down to half a bagel a day, dry. But I'm not happy about it. Bill Lawrence has gone up two sizes in his pants and is now a 38. "I'm willing to go to 40, boss. I know what's at stake."

It's great to see a young man who knows what's important. Having lost the breakfast skirmish, the young business guy now decides to come after the evening meal. He sees some potential savings there if we cut back on starches and desserts. Not the whole $250,000, he admits, but some significant savings. He then hands me a list of restaurants that are too costly and are no longer approved for our rewrite-night dinners.

I get menus from all those restaurants and have them laminated and put into a book. From now on we will order dinner *only* from those restaurants. And everyone will add an extra steak to whatever dinner they were planning to order.

"I'm a vegetarian," Amy complains.

"Give it to Bill," I tell her.

The staff has had an average weight gain of four pounds at this point, and cholesterol issues are also now beginning to surface. No one said this would be easy. But the rewrite dinner is sacred. I view it as a reward for all the hard work these kids are putting in. I want it to be fun. I want it to be special. And now, I also want it to be very, very expensive.

Having been unable to disrupt our supply lines, the young business whiz now turns his attention to our transportation unit, where he thinks we might prove more vulnerable.

"Why do the writers get to go home in taxis?" he wants to know. "Why can't they take the subway?"

"Well, they're usually leaving work at three thirty or four in the morning. The nearest subway's about ten blocks away through some rough neighborhoods. I'd be a little nervous about it as a safety issue."

"They could walk in pairs."

I can see him doing the math in his head.

OK, maybe we lose a writer or two. We can replace them. Maybe with someone cheaper. Maybe someone who doesn't like bagels.

He feels he has to make a stand somewhere. Get some concessions he can send back to headquarters in Burbank.

"OK. I'll authorize payment for taxis," he relents. "But only for taxis taken after midnight. Before midnight the writers have to take the subway."

I agree to this taxi compromise because no writer has ever left the office before midnight anyway, and if they ever did, they'd be so deliriously happy they would float home on air. And although neither of us realizes it, at that moment, much as the Treaty of Versailles paved the way for the World War II, our transportation agreement will create the conditions that will culminate in the final battle in the Condiment Wars.

It all comes to a head early the next week when the guy refuses to reimburse Timmy Hobert for a taxi ride home when Timmy got into the cab at eleven fifteen in the morning. Timmy had stayed and worked all through the previous day and night and was essentially punching out after a thirty-six-hour shift on the morning of the *next* day. He should have been entitled to a helicopter.

"The policy is clear," the guy explains. "No taxi reimbursement during daylight hours."

I give him one last chance to save his job.

"It's twenty-three bucks. Don't you think you ought to make an exception?"

"You either have a policy or you don't."

"You're fired," I tell him.

"I work for Katzenberg," he tells me. "You can't fire me."

"Wanna bet?" I tell him.

I call Jeffrey in California and I offer him a very simple choice. Not hostile. Not angry. Easy decision for him to make. Strictly business. He can have this guy here in New York. Or he can have me. He can't have both of us. And believe me, I'm fine either way.

Jeffrey thinks about it for a full second and a half. The guy will be gone in the morning. And thus, with a whimper and not a bang, the Condiment Wars come to an end. I won. How come it doesn't make me feel better?

The "wars," while a pleasant-enough diversion, cannot, of course, obscure the real battle that is taking place. The one between me and Mike. We fight about everything. We fight with the ferocity that only people who have once been in love know how to fight. We know the weaknesses. We know what hurts. That's where we go.

"You shut me out. You don't listen. You care about the writers more than you care about me,"—from Mike.

"You don't trust me. You don't listen. You only care about yourself,"—from me.

"You don't love me anymore,"—from both of us.

When I awake, I'm still seated in my chair overlooking Central Park. The sun has stepped in and replaced the moon. Nina Simone is silent. The wine bottle's somehow empty. I check the fax machine. The script is just coming in, the pages are still hot. It's nine thirty A.M. The writers stayed all night.

I shower. Make coffee. Read the changed script. Some very nice work. Not perfect, but a big leap forward, and it's only Wednesday. We don't shoot till Friday. This staff could turn out *War and Peace* between now and then. I decide to head over to the studio. Check with Mike, see how he liked the changes.

I stop by the writers' offices first. The conference room is empty. There's a blizzard of paper piled up in the corners. I cross over to Bill's office. The door's closed. There's a big sign posted on it: QUIET. IDIOT SLEEPING. Scotch-taped underneath, a Polaroid of Bill in a terry-cloth bathrobe.

I make my way down to the stage, which is strangely silent and empty. This should be the middle of rehearsal. I find one of the ADs.

"What's up? Where is everyone?"

"Mike didn't like the script, so he went home."

"He just went home?"

"Yeah."

I walk out the studio door, hail a cab, and head out to the airport. I have a home too. It's in California. And that's where I'm going.

About an hour and a half into the flight, I call Bill. He's a little sleepy, but after a few tentative coughs, he finds his voice. All eager and golden retriever puppyish.

"Hey, Gar, how's it goin'? How'd Mike like the rewrite?"

"Bill, I'm over Chicago."

"That doesn't sound like a good thing."

I explain to Bill what happened. The empty stage. Mike gone home.

"I'm heading to L.A, and I'm not coming back. The show's yours."

"Fuck the show. How're you doin'?"

Somebody raised this boy up right.

"Don't worry about me, I'm fine. But you have to step up now and take over. It's important."

"You should come back. C'mon. Go tell the pilot to turn the plane around. They'll do that for you. You're big."

"Here's what's going to happen. Katzenberg will call you first. He won't say anything bad about me, but he'll already have moved on. That's only right. There's a lot at stake. He has to protect the show. The network guys will follow with their own phone calls shortly after Katzenberg's."

I'm sounding a lot like Marlon Brando in *The Godfather* now, I realize.

"Don't worry about what they say about me. Don't feel you have to defend me. Just get ready to take over."

"Mike won't let this happen."

"I really think this is what he wants, Bill. I don't know what else to do."

"I'll call Mike."

"No, don't. This will all work out for the best, you'll see."

"OK."

"And there's a lesson here. You may as well learn it now. It's one of the few unshakable truths about show business."

"What's that?"

"You fight with a star, you lose. Always was. Always will be."

"Fight with a star, lose. Got it.

"Take care, Bill."

"Call me when you're over Denver."

{chapter twenty-two}

*B*ack in Los Angeles now, there's a flurry of activity. Katzenberg calls. He's at his best in these situations. Honest. Grown-up. Always trying to be positive and move forward.

"You won't be happy if you quit."

Jeffrey knows the power of that word for me.

"I don't think I'm quitting. It feels to me like I'm being moved out."

"Mike's upset too. He thinks you walked out on him."

"What else is new?"

Jamie Tarses, the young president of ABC, calls. Jamie's been great through all this. Which just means that she agrees with me, I guess. She really feels that the darker shades of Mike Flaherty's character are turning viewers off. Especially women eighteen to thirty-four, the holy grail of the TV-viewing audience.

"We'll split the cost of the shutdown with DreamWorks. We'd like this to resolve with you back in New York, though, running the show."

"That's a generous offer, thanks. And I think we can make back some of the deficit by cutting down on bagels. At least, that's what I've been told."

I meet with Skip Brittenham. Skip's not only my attorney now, he's also Michael's. He also represents DreamWorks. And he represents ABC. Only in America. Only Skip. He's also my friend.

"I set up a call between you and Mike today at five. I've heard his side. I know your side. Either you guys find a solution, or you don't go back. You're both miserable."

At home, Diana, while clearly wanting me to be happy, is, at the same time, very sympathetic to Michael's point of view, and won't whisper a negative thought about him.

She loves Michael and feels protective of him, and she's struggling to remain neutral. This neutrality, while laudable in a country like Switzerland, I find annoying in my own wife.

"You have such a long and loving history with Mike. Maybe you need to try and see things more from his point of view."

"Oh, do I? See, I didn't know that."

"We'll talk about it tomorrow. When you're a little older. And a little more mature."

Once, somebody asked us what our secret was, as a couple—how we stayed together all these years.

"I'm easy to live with," I replied, with all sincerity, only to turn around and see that Diana had fallen off her chair and was on the floor, laughing hysterically. So perhaps not.

Mike and I speak on the phone. He says it was all a misunderstanding. He had a doctor's appointment. Forgot to tell the AD. Was surprised that I'd leave like that. He didn't like the rewrite, true, and he didn't want to rehearse it. So with the doctor's appointment, he thought he'd go do that and then come back and meet with me and the writers.

I apologize if I misunderstood. But, I state the obvious.

"Look we're both miserable here," I offer, and Mike makes no attempt to disagree.

We set up a meeting for later that week, in New York, to see if we can get things back on track. We both say we're sorry. And I think we're both sincere. But at this point, who knows what that even means.

We meet at Sarabeth's Kitchen on the Upper East Side, near Mike's apartment. It's a nursery book of a place. Cute and comfortable inside. Lots of bright colors and heavy fabrics. It really does look like a little girl's playhouse. I wonder if a lot of couples come here to break up. It would be hard to make a scene amid all this raspberry jam.

We're shown to a table upstairs where we can be alone and no one will bother us. I order oatmeal, which I think is the most non-threatening food item on the menu. Mike counters with a carrot muffin. If there's going to be food fight, at least no one will get hurt.

We each take out our list of grievances. I have mine on a three-by-five card. Mike takes out a yellow legal pad. And as he articulates his position, for the first time I begin to get a clear idea of just how wide the chasm is between what had been his expectations for *Spin City* and what has been his reality. And how much he believes I have betrayed him.

"We're supposed to be equal partners," he begins, "but you make a lot of decisions unilaterally."

"During a show week, a lot of decisions are time-sensitive," I try to explain. "I don't want to stop rehearsal to ask if you want blue drapes or tan drapes in the conference room scene."

"But I want you to. I want you to call me about stuff like that. I want you to call me about everything."

"I'm just trying to help make things easier. You have a pretty full job there playing Mike Flaherty, don't you think?"

"I don't want you to help me. I don't want you to make things easier. I want to do all this."

"OK, I'll try to remember to be more inclusive."

"I want to sign off on the budgets, too. I should be there when they make them up."

"Jeez, even the guys who're makin' up the budgets don't want to be there when they're makin' up the budgets. They want *my* job, or yours. They're only makin' up the budgets so that someday they won't have to."

"I don't care. I'm the executive producer too. And I should be there."

To me, it's like hooking Secretariat up to a milk wagon. But sure. OK. In fact, if Mike's going to be there, maybe I don't have to be.

The list continues through the oatmeal and the carrot muffin, through several cups of mint tea and an assortment of precious little powdered white cookies. Mike's list is long and detailed. Some of the points are trivial. Some sting with their accuracy and insight.

Mike complains that the show's too long. We shoot too many pages and then whole scenes and subplots have to be dropped in editing in order to get down to time. I counter that the extra length allows me to edit to a very fast pace. Keep the energy up. Keep the New York City feeling alive.

But I think he has a real point here. And I can understand his frustration. Diana, in another of her annoyingly perceptive observations, has pointed out that perhaps I make sure I have so much time in the editing room because that's the one place I still have complete control. Gee, it must be nice to be so highly evolved.

At the end of all of this, there is one central thought that's really bothering Mike: I don't respect him as a full partner. I still see him as an actor—a young actor whom I discovered. And I'm not willing to face the fact that he's grown up and entitled to a full seat at the table now. In my heart, I don't believe that's true. That I'm just trying to do my job. But I also think I'm easy to live with, so perhaps I'm not the best judge.

The problem is that, at this point in his career, Mike is certainly entitled to have things done exactly the way he wants. And he's entitled to have his vision of the show realized. *Spin City* would never have gotten on the air in the first place if it weren't for Mike. No network really wanted to do a show set in New York City. No network really wanted to do a show based in the political arena.

But all three networks wanted to work with Mike Fox, so that was a fairly short discussion.

"You guys really want to do a show set in New York City in the mayor's office? Cause we hate that idea."

"Yeah, that's what we want to do."

"And Mike Fox is in it?"

"Mm-hm."

"OK."

I'm aware of how much of this success is owed to Mike. I know we're all lucky to be working with such a talented actor. And I've said many times to the writers that they need to make sure they stop and enjoy this.

"You're working with one of the all-time great comic actors. You're in the Super Bowl, and you might not get back here again so quick."

But funneling every aspect of the show through Mike, I believe, is inherently dangerous. Basically, what will happen is that *Spin City* will become only *his* creative experience. All the rest of us will be trying to hit a moving target, with only Mike, the star actor, able to tell us when we've hit it. I realize a lot of shows and most movies operate that way, but I can't figure out a place for myself in that world. Trying to implement someone else's vision.

I work best from a small personal thought. Throw that pebble in the water. Watch the ripples flow out from there and hope it's something that will interest people waiting on the shore. This other way of working is like polling the people on the shore about what they want, throwing a rock to that spot, and starting off there. I don't know how to do that. Or why I would want to.

Mike and I are both now over the legal limit for herbal tea. And it's not possible, at this point, for us to have any more cookies or anything more to say. So, with everything laid out on the table, we decide we can, and want to, finish out the year together. We agree that we'll each try harder to be good partners. That we'll listen more and listen better.

The air is clear. We're starting over. We hug. I pick up the check. My treat. Mike says he wants to pay. His treat. We decide to split it. The new era begins.

{ c h a p t e r t w e n t y - t h r e e }

*F*our weeks have gone by since the meeting with Mike. I'm back in my apartment. It's four A.M. I'm in my chair. I have my wine. I'm listening to Miles Davis. Never a good sign. Means I'm feeling dark and angry. Dissonant. Confrontational. Of all the artists who played the Village Gate, Miles Davis was the one I always found to be most personally unpleasant.

"You. Get me a ginger ale," he would bark in that raspy voice, at whichever unfortunate one of us waiters was close at hand. No denying his genius. Just a man who I never saw smile. Who I never heard say "thank you" or "please."

The nicest man who ever played the Gate was John Lewis, the leader of the Modern Jazz Quartet. An elegant, soft-spoken gentleman, he would often sit in the kitchen betweens sets, sipping from a glass of ginger ale he had gotten for himself, and kibbitz with the waiters as we scurried about our tasks.

The most memorable performer, without a doubt, was Nina Simone. Very few performers could sell out all three shows, with that last show starting sometimes around one A.M. Nina Simone was a glorious exception, who not only sold out all three shows but brought in the big spenders, as well.

There was always an air of danger around her performances and around Nina Simone herself. An air of unpredictability, of volatility. I saw her play sets that lasted an hour; I saw her play sets that lasted fifteen minutes. I saw her walk off stage once midsong, when, after she had finished chastening an unruly crowd, a woman in the audience called back to Nina, "Kiss my black ass." And all I could think of as she left the stage was, *no way this is good for my tips.*

I listen to Miles Davis for a few more minutes. Then I get up and take the CD off. Don't want to go there. And I put on Modern Jazz Quartet. Immediately, I feel more elegant and dignified. I pour myself another glass of wine and resume my perch overlooking the sleeping city below.

I love this apartment. And I remember it was Michael Fox who found this place for us. He was so excited about me coming to New York. And so concerned that I have a good time here that he started going out with Realtors looking at apartments for me. I was at home in Los Angeles when the phone rang. The voice on the other end was vibrating with excitement.

"Hi, this is Debbie Strickland from Strickland Realty in New York."

"Uh-huh."

"I'm here with Michael J. Fox, and he would like to speak with you."

"OK."

"Michael J. Fox, the actor."

"I know who he is."

"I mean it's really him. It's really Michael J. Fox."

"Can you put him on please?"

"OK."

Mike gets on.

"Gar, I've known you a long time. I know you and Diana. And I know I'm standing in your apartment."

He tells me about it. Right on Central Park. Thirteen floors up. Gorgeous views.

"Sounds great."

"Problem is, it won't be here tomorrow. Someone's going to take it if you don't. You have to come now."

"OK."

Debbie the Realtor comes back on. I tell her we're on our way to New York and we're going to make an offer on this apartment. "Don't let anyone else buy it before we get there."

"OK," she says.

Then, as if she still can't believe it herself: "That was Michael J. Fox."

I know that Mike and I are both trying very hard now to be better partners. I know that. And I appreciate all his efforts. But we still can't seem to break out of the roles we're trapped in. He still sees me as shutting him out or including him only reluctantly. And through my very tired and very frustrated eyes, it seems everything we write for Mike is received first with suspicion. His first instinct is to put up barriers and deconstruct. And question. And judge. "Make it better. Make it different. Just make it something else."

Tonight Bill and I were working late, just the two of us. We kept writing and rewriting this same scene. It was about two thirty A.M., and we weren't getting anywhere, which is unusual for us when we write together. We usually knock out two or three scenes before the coffee's finished brewing.

"Why are we rewriting this?" I ask Bill, who's younger and may actually remember why. "This scene completely works. I like it."

"I like it too."

"Then why are we rewriting?"

There's a beat of silence.

"Mike didn't like it."

So, I come home, pour some wine, put on Miles Davis, and sulk.

In January, Mike wins the Golden Globe for Best Actor in a Comedy, and that buys us a couple of weeks or so of trust, but that bubble bursts pretty quickly. I think maybe Mike feels he won because he pushed us into making the character more weird and dark. In our hearts, Bill and I feel maybe he won because we pushed him a step, or maybe half a step, back into the light. In any case, the mutual frustration quickly reasserts itself.

It's so strange. Here we are, on the verge of a megamillion-dollar syndication deal. The ratings are strong, and the pickup for the third season is imminent. Mike's the funniest guy in the land, certified by the Hollywood Foreign Press. And yet, for the first time in my career, I'm not excited about the thought of going in to work. There seems to be a gray cloud hanging over the whole show.

There's also another cloud hanging over all of us now, though we don't know it yet. An angry black cloud that will drench us and ultimately engulf Michael and his entire family.

It begins simply enough. Mike is absent a lot. Or late. There are a lot of doctor's appointments. A lot of tests. Mike seems tired a lot. We keep the schedule flexible. Work around the times he needs to rest. There seems to be some confusion in the medical world as to what exactly this may be. So much frustration on Mike's part. So little anyone can do, it seems, to be of any help. They're torturing this guy with all these tests. And then, for the first time, we hear the word—Parkinson's.

Jeffrey comes to New York. Skip comes too. We meet in Mike's office, and he lays it out. He's very straightforward. Not an ounce of self-pity. I'm impressed by his quiet courage. His absolute certainty that he'll prevail.

At this point, we're the only ones who know, and Mike would like for it to stay that way. It's the early stages of the disease. The doctors have some protocols they want to try. They believe Mike can continue working for at least three or four more years, with only some slight adjustments to his workload. Mike wants to keep working. He wants to keep doing *Spin City.* That's crucial to him.

No one else speaks at first. This is the longest I've ever seen Katzenberg be silent in my life. Or Skip. Both of those guys, razor-sharp and smart, usually have four solutions to any problem by now. They have nothing to offer. Neither do I. Other than love, and respect, and understanding.

We go back to work, the official party line being suspicion of Lyme disease. Mike has a port implanted in his arm to accommodate the daily intravenous fluids he's receiving. He's unbelievably upbeat and determined to continue to live normally. But the frustration is inevitable, and understandable, as we crawl toward the end of the year.

Parkinson's will cut short Mike's brilliant career. Then miraculously put him on a path where he will become a symbol of hope and courage and commitment. A spiritual leader to millions of people suffering from neurodegenerative diseases. And it will become Mike's lifework to help eradicate this cruel disease.

We do, in fact, receive our pickup early for the third year. Mike gets nominated for an Emmy. The syndication bids come in from New York, Los Angeles, and Chicago. They are way higher than what we could have expected or dreamed of. But there is nothing that can get us out from underneath this cloud.

With the end of the second season, and the official pickup for the third now in hand, I have a big decision to make about my future. My contract calls for me to be in New York for the first two years only. After that, I have the option to return to New York, or I can stay home in Los Angeles. In either case, I will receive the same exact salary.

This will not be an easy decision to make. On the one hand, I'm extremely tired, not really any happier, and Bill Lawrence is a superstar in the making and seems more than ready to step up and take over. On the other hand, I don't want Mike to think I'm abandoning him. We aren't sure what the ramifications of his illness are going to be, but even in the best case, it seems certain he'll need more rest, more care, and more attention. If he feels he needs me, I want to be there for him. Turns out the decision will be made for me.

Skip Brittenham has asked me to lunch. He seems a little subdued, but I chalk that up to my own tiredness more than anything else.

"I received a letter from Mike," Skip says over coffee and dessert. "Well, it's more than a letter. I think you need to respond to it."

He takes out a really large envelope that contains a six- or seven-page document, typed, single-spaced. The heading is "Michael J. Fox: Manifesto."*

"Whoa. Last time someone issued one of those Russia collapsed."

Skip begins to read, "Item one: Michael Fox will have final say on all writers to be hired. Item two: All story ideas will be submitted to Michael Fox for his approval. Item three . . ."

"No need to go on to item three, Skip. I'm out."

There follow a series of angry faxes between Michael and myself. We're back to square one. A rerun of our whole time in New York. A friendship of fifteen years. The two of us like brothers. It's over. Just like that, it's over. Michael and I will not exchange a single word for almost a year.

---

*Years later, Mike insisted he had never written that. Some assistant had put it on there as a working title for herself, and it mistakenly stayed on the draft that Skip received.

1998

{ c h a p t e r t w e n t y - f o u r }

I've always believed that whenever someone starts off by saying, "Let me be frank" or "I'll be honest," what follows will inevitably be neither frank nor honest. But if I look back, more than a decade ago, to that confusing *Spin City* portion of my life, if I try to apportion blame to either me or to Mike, I honestly believe, speaking frankly and in all seriousness, I was more at fault than Mike. And I didn't respond with the kindness and thoughtfulness that I should have brought to the situation.

I'm not a psychiatrist, and evidently I'm not easy to live with, but maybe I did feel some resentment at having to share "power" with someone who had, at one time, been a kind of protégé of mine. On some level, perhaps, I must have felt he was disloyal. Was placing himself above the team. Cardinal sins in the world I grew up in, and still inhabit in my mind.

I know I resented having to work far away from home. Resented being away from Diana and the kids. And since that's the third time I've used the term *resentment,* perhaps I was indeed harboring some. I don't know. I didn't think so at the time. But whatever clarity or perspective I might eventually bring to bear on that situation would still be far away in the future.

It's New Year's Eve, 1998, and Diana and I are celebrating by staying home. We had been up in Utah skiing and had planned to have a big New Year's party there. But Diana wasn't feeling well, so we came home early. We thought it might be altitude-related. Maybe a reaction to the stress of the Archer situation. We weren't overly concerned. Just being cautious.

This has been a particularly tense time in the history of the Archer school. After a year of lawsuits and countersuits and appeals, all of which we've won, we are now coming up on the city council vote. This will be the final word. I've promised Diana we'll have that fourteen million dollars when the time comes. And for some reason she believes me.

We've rented *Saturday Night Fever,* brought in some pizza, and cozied up by the fire. And tonight, Diana does seem a little better. But she falls asleep before Travolta even gets to put his white suit on.

I turn on the east-coast satellite feed at nine o'clock. And I raise a toast to this new year of 1998, little knowing that it will be the most difficult year of my life.

Diana is ill. Perhaps gravely ill. For the first time in our house, there are prescription bottles with her name on them. This is serious. And it seems to have happened overnight.

Diana, who has never had a headache. Never missed a day of teaching. Never had a checkup. Never had a regular doctor.

It was always a joke between us. I have eleven doctors on call at any given moment. I have had fourteen major operations. I don't quite enjoy surgery. That would be overstating. But I like to take advantage of the new technology. I'm partial to Demerol. And I mend quickly. But this, whatever Diana's going through . . . this is no joke.

She is suddenly incredibly tired and weak. She has difficulty eating and swallowing. Difficulty keeping food down. Then, in rapid succession, difficulty walking, difficulty sitting up, difficulty staying awake.

She insists on trying to control this herself. She's relying on natural herbs and prayer and meditation. There's also music that's involved in this "cure," some annoyingly "soothing" music that sounds like Ravi Shankar on Quaaludes.

Diana is not improving. In fact, she's getting worse. And so is the fuckin' music. Finally, she agrees to see a doctor. A guy whose name she was given from one of her spiritual-guide-type girlfriends, who disdain medical science and believe broccoli will cure everything. Broccoli and massage.

In the doctor's waiting room, they're playing the same Ravi Shankar on Quaaludes tape we have at home. This does not augur well. When we meet the guy, he seems OK. And I'm sure if you want to go shopping or take in a movie, he might make an excellent companion. But we're looking for a doctor here.

He's wearing cowboy boots. I don't think you should wear cowboy boots unless you're on a horse. I ask him about doing some tests.

"Tests can be very misleading," he tells me. "They're also invasive. I think we should go slowly."

Yeah, well my wife's disintegrating before my eyes, so I don't know how slowly we can go. But, Diana's comfortable with this approach. He does agree, however, to do one blood test. That will tell him a lot, he says. Diana gives blood. I don't get orange juice, or a shower. And we go home.

When we return to get the results, this time he's not wearing cowboy boots. He's wearing moccasins. I don't like getting medical-test results from a guy in moccasins. He seems concerned. Some very high numbers in the CPK and the sed rate. Some problems with white-blood-cell count. He actually seems scared. I know I am. The only one who doesn't seem worried is Diana.

"Rodeo Doc" wants us to see a friend of his who specializes in autoimmune problems. He's in the same building, and he can see us now, if we want to go over. We go up two floors to see the autoimmune guy. He's wearing sensible shoes, which I like, but he seems to have no other patients. Actually, there's no one else, at all, in the office. Not a secretary. Not a nurse. Some nice art work, but no other humans. I like that he has so much time to spend with us. But why?

He's from South Africa. Johannesburg. Really misses his old

country. He's had trouble integrating into the medical community here. Very closed society. Very competitive. Some things were better in South Africa. Yeah, but we don't have apartheid here, OK? And how about we talk about the tests?

Basically, he's stumped. He prescribes some stuff I never heard of, and Diana signs up for some massage treatments. And a guy from New Zealand comes to the house with some kind of electromagnetic machine that makes a lot of noise—but does sound better than the Shankar tapes, anyway.

After two weeks of this, I can't take it anymore.

"I want you to go to a doctor. A real doctor. With regular shoes and at least one foot in the real world of American medicine."

"This is my illness," she tells me. "I want to deal with it in my own way."

"It's not just *your* illness," I respond one day, out of frustration and now anger. "I'm your husband. I'm your partner. I love you. And, you have two daughters who love you and need you."

Reluctantly, Diana agrees to let me find a doctor. A close and dear friend, Marilyn Bergman, recommends Dr. Allan Metzger, at Cedars Sinai. And for that, and so many other kindnesses, I'm forever in her debt.

At this point, Diana's reduced to being in a wheelchair, and as I wheel her into Dr. Metzger's office for our first meeting, we're greeted by a man who exudes competence and compassion. I take a deep breath and allow myself a little exhale. But just for a minute. And just for one breath.

Dr. Metzger explains that for whatever reason, and one we may never actually learn, Diana's immune system has basically gone haywire and is overproducing collagen at an alarming rate. If this can't be stopped and then reversed, theoretically the collagen could spread into vital organs and be fatal. The problem is, suppressing the immune system has its own risks. And the weakened body is susceptible to all kinds of infections and other invasions. It's going to be a delicate balancing act.

When I'm alone with Dr. Metzger, I try to fill him in a little bit about his new patient. He possesses the rare ability, for a doctor, of being a very good listener. I explain Diana's resistance to doctors. How on some level, I know, she regards it as *her* failure that she's become someone's patient. I ask him to always give me the whole range of outcomes and options, but not to necessarily share those with Diana. She and I have spoken about this, and she doesn't want to know. She wants to focus on her meditations. And she's designated me to be the "information guy" and share stuff with her, or not, at my discretion.

Dr. Metzger outlines his plan of attack. We're going to have to do some tests. A lot of tests. Some will be difficult for Diana, but he feels he needs every scrap of information he can get. He wants to bring in a colleague, Dr. Phil Clements at UCLA, who's the leading expert in the United States on scleroderma, which would be an almost worst-case diagnosis but can't be ruled out. There are also indications of possible lupus and polymyositis that he needs to explore.

"There's one thing you need to know," he tells me.

"What's that?"

"It's probably going to get worse before it gets better."

"Is it going to get better?"

He looks at me, I see him making the decision.

"I don't know."

"I appreciate the honesty."

He gives me his card, and on the back he writes his home number and his cell phone number.

"Call me day or night. Anything you think I need to know. Anything you need to know. Call me."

I want to hug Dr. Metzger, but I'm not sure it's appropriate. We've just met. And then, without thinking, I find that I'm around the other side of his desk and I'm giving him a big, long hug. He hugs me back. Diana is wheeled back into the room.

"He must've been a ballplayer, huh?"

Dr. Metzger's right about one thing. It's getting worse. And the tests are indeed difficult. Painful, even. At UCLA, Diana has to have a CAT-scan with her arms outstretched over her head. One problem: Diana can't raise her arms above her head. And even if I raise them for her, she can't maintain that position.

The only solution is for me to hold her arms outstretched and run in the opposite direction while she goes through the machine. I'm given a lead-lined outfit to wear, which weighs about twenty-five pounds and is reinforced with an extra "lead loincloth" to cover one's private parts. I appreciate the extra protection. And I have to admit, it's very slimming.

The technician gives me the sign that she's ready to begin. And as Diana lies there, with me holding her arms above her head, the machine starts to move her forward. At the same time, I'm going in the opposite direction and forcing Diana's arms to remain outstretched over her head. Diana's screaming because it hurts so much, and the technician stops the test. We get back into starting position. Take a breath. We'll try again.

We do two or three more attempts but break it off each time. I don't know what to do. I know Dr. Metzger wants this test. Diana's eyes are bleary from pain. I'm dripping in my lead tuxedo.

"I can't do this. It hurts too much."

"One more try. If we don't get it, we'll quit."

"Promise."

"Promise."

We make one adjustment. I cross over to the other side. Diana feels stronger on the left for some reason. She thinks we'll have a better chance.

"Deep breath."

"Deep breath."

"I love you."

"I love you."

The machine starts up again. We resume our crazy dance. Diana slides through the machine and we get the pictures we need. I look up at the technician in the booth. She is crying. But she gives me the thumbs up.

At St. Johns, where we are sent for yet another series of CAT-scans, we meet our first and only nasty person. A sadistic male nurse. I wasn't in the room with Diana for these tests, but when she came out, she was white. She said this guy was mean and kept pushing her into a position, even though she kept telling him she couldn't do that and how much it hurt. He told her to "stop complaining."

There was an older woman seated next to Diana. "He did the same to me," she said, looking shriveled and helpless in her bathrobe.

Without realizing it, I'm running down the hall into the nurse's room to find this guy. As I push open the door, at the outer reaches of my craziness, I hear a woman's voice.

"Sir, you can't go in there."

I see the guy standing there by his locker. I grab him by the throat and start pounding his head into the locker.

"Hey, what the fuck . . . ?"

"Stop complaining," I'm screaming. "You tell my wife to stop complaining. You scare little old women."

Some other people are coming in now, trying to separate us. I realize how much I want to feel this guy's head go through the plate-glass window. If I can just move him over to the window and put his head through the glass, everything will be all right. All the rage, and all the anger, all the impotent, helpless feelings I have will disappear.

I hear an alarm go off, and I hear someone call for "security." And I realize they must be calling about me. I look at this guy who I want to kill.

"You need to get yourself another fuckin' job," I tell him.

But I doubt he's open to receiving career counseling from me at this moment.

During all this, Diana is brave. Heroic, even. But continuing to slide. She's losing more mobility. And now she's virtually unable to swallow any food. Swallowing is not a reflex, as I always thought, bearing in mind that after thirteen years of college I was still short that one unit of biology. Perhaps they covered swallowing in that class.

Swallowing requires a muscle and Diana's has weakened to the point that it's barely functioning. All she can handle, it seems, is sushi, mashed avocado, and cottage cheese.

"If you bring me cottage cheese again I will throw it at you," she informs me one day.

"You can't lift your arms," I point out.

But I drop cottage cheese from the menu, replacing it with Jell-O. Always a crowd-pleaser.

I cut the sushi into incredibly tiny pieces, line her throat with mint oil, and shovel it in as best I can. Diana likes to "bark" after a successful feeding. And I do give her a snout a little rub as a reward.

Dr. Metzger calls us to his office. He's gathered up the test results. He's consulted with Dr. Clements, and he has a plan. He draws a diagram that looks like a little bit like the Olympic rings, three of them overlapping and connecting.

"Basically, we've got a little bit of everything going on," he begins. "One day it's more scleroderma, one day, lupus, the next, polymyositis. Then back to lupus. You may as well call this Diana Meehan's disease," he tells us.

Dr. Metzger's plan is aggressive. And, it's bold. He's going to treat it, basically, as if it were cancer. Chemotherapy in the Cancer Center at Cedars. Cycles of infusions, three days a week, every three weeks. Here we go.

{ chapter twenty-five }

T here is an air of competence at the Cedars Sinai Cancer Center. And of remarkable caring and concern. The nurses, the whole time we're there, are somehow consistently upbeat and kind. I don't know what planet these people come from, but if I saw wings coming out from underneath those uniforms, I wouldn't be surprised.

The days are grueling, especially at the beginning, as Diana's tolerances are being determined. Basically, she's being given poison in an IV drip, and it has to be controlled and directed in its fury. There are usually three different varieties involved. I've thankfully lost all memory of their actual names. When the first one goes through, the first time, Diana tells me she can actually feel it traveling all through her body.

The dosage is dispersed agonizingly slowly at first to see what she can handle. That first day, we're at the center for eight hours. Coming home that night, we don't even try to make it upstairs to bed; we just fall out in the living room. It seems like we've been gone a month.

Somehow, unbelievably, these visits to the cancer center settle into a routine. They have recognizable rhythms and "seasons." They become our life. Three long days every three weeks. Diana's usually wiped out for at least three days after each treatment. She's basically asleep one week out of every three.

There's a dizzying array of pill bottles in the house now. Many of the pills are simply there to counteract the impact and effect of other pills. It's a real balancing act, with the big gun here being prednisone, which Diana is taking now at 75 mg to start. There are some other exotic entries in the pill derby, including Cell Cept, which was developed in the organ-transplant program.

Diana asks about side effects. I tell her there won't be any. That's what she wants to hear. And that's what she believes. In point of fact, the possible side effects are so confusing and possibly so debilitating that it hardly makes any sense, I feel, to even get started on them.

Diana is now eighty-four pounds and cannot keep her head up. There's nothing she can do by herself anymore. I have to feed her. Wash her. Escort her to the bathroom. I have to carry her from room to room. Carry her downstairs. Carry her back up at night. Carry her from the bed to the den, where she's set up her "camp" on a couch with a view of the garden.

I tell her of my plans to turn the upstairs into a hospital for her. I want all the equipment. I want nurses around the clock. I want to hire doctors to sit by, on call, in case we need them. Diana doesn't want any of that.

"I want you to do it," she tells me. "Just you."

"I can't," I tell her. "It's too much."

"No, it's not. You can do it."

She doesn't want that hospital "energy" in the house. This is where we live. This is our home. She doesn't want the kids to have these kinds of associations with the house they've grown up in.

"It'll be an adventure for us," she goes on. "I know I'm going to get better. And in the end, when this is all done, we'll be glad we went through this."

"I don't need this adventure," I tell her.

And I don't tell her what I also believe now. That I'm not so sure this is going to turn out well. Neither is Dr. Metzger.

Everyone we know, it seems, steps up to help. So many people who love Diana. Who've always looked up to her. Admired her indomitable spirit. Who're crushed and confused and heartbroken to see her in distress.

Katzenberg is great. He tells me not to come back into work until Diana's better. Says he'll "kick my ass" if he sees me in the office. I have Jeffrey by about 150 pounds, but he's wiry and determined. I don't doubt he can do it.

At this point, Diana can't hold a newspaper, or even focus on the TV for any extended period of time. I become her source of news and information and entertainment. She calls me the "cute little CNN guy," as I come in to do headlines in the morning. And some fluff features, too, I must admit.

I try to pick out good news. Clip out recipes. Anything to do with rescued pets. For the first time in my life, I understand the appeal of Eyewitness News.

At night, after I tuck Diana in, I step out on the balcony to say my prayers. I make the usual deals with God that anyone in my position always makes. All the things I'll do. All the things I'll stop doing, if only Diana will get better.

I thank the universe for all the kindness shown so far. I thank my parents and my grandparents. I thank my ancestors. I hope they're pleased with me. With my behavior. I ask the universe for one thing. To let me walk outside again with Diana arm-in-arm, one time. And to see the wind blow through her hair. That's all I want. Give me that, you'll never hear from me again.

I sleep on a mat at the foot of the bed. Or sometimes sitting in the chair across the room. Diana's sleep is fitful, and sometimes if I roll over or cough or snore, which allegedly, from time to time, I have done, it will wake her.

Sometimes Diana wakes gasping for air, and my blood turns to ice to hear those painful, helpless gurgles. There are two times it's so bad, I'm sure she won't still be with us in the morning. Only one time does Diana ever complain. After a scary round of gasping and gulping, dripping with sweat, eyes rimmed red from exhaustion, she says, "It's not fair."

"No, it's not."

"Trade me in," she says. "Get yourself another model. A younger one."

"No, thanks, I like the one I rode in with. And don't ever say that again, OK? It hurts my feelings."

"It's always about you, isn't it?"

And we laugh. Incredibly, we laugh.

Small victories. I take Diana for a "walk." We go out the back door and walk twenty feet around to the front door. She can't lift her feet up high enough to step up onto the welcome mat, which I kick away. She's exhausted from the "hike." But there's a small flicker of accomplishment there at the corner of her still-beautiful smile. She naps for five hours after.

I have a lot of help. My assistant, Heather Green, is a gracious and generous presence in our life. She's the "meet and greet" at the hospital. We have it down. I pop the trunk as soon as we land, and Heather crosses to the back and takes out the wheelchair. By the time I get Diana out of the passenger seat, Heather has the wheelchair ready, she wheels it over, and we slide Diana in. Heather's already checked inside the center to make sure the bed is ready and the medicine is waiting. Always with a gentle smile.

Betsy Nolan, Cailin's nanny, is also a lifeline. She's been with our family since Cailin was born in 1983. And somehow, she's still Cailin's nanny, even though Cailin is fifteen and has her learner's permit. Betsy has, in effect, become our third daughter. A natural caregiver and caretaker, she has accepted her promotion to "substitute mother/father" with consummate grace.

Cailin's being shut out here, I know. I just can't seem to manage all these different roles well. My attention's all on Diana. And I seem to have very little left over to be Cailin's father too. I know she resents it. Thank God for Betsy.

Diana's spiritual guide-lady group also steps up big time. They are there with food. They are there with books to read to Diana. They are there with massage oils and crystals and tea. A lot of tea.

On Saturday mornings, they come early to give me half a day off so I can see my friends and go play basketball. They say they're letting me out so I can go to church.

Dr. Metzger calls every day to check in. Once a week, we go over to his office so he can see Diana for himself.

"He likes to kick my tires," Diana says.

Some of the numbers are improving. Some are staying the same. None are getting worse, which he thinks is a very good sign. Diana's still confined to a wheelchair for these visits. Her stroller, she calls it. But she's sitting up straighter now, and Dr. Metzger congratulates her on her "posture."

"I'll call my mother. She'll be very happy. She always wanted me to sit up straight. Like a lady."

Actually, the calls to, and from, Diana's parents have been anything but happy. Diana doesn't want them to know the full extent of what she's going through. Doesn't want them to come down to see her in this condition. I bear the brunt of their anger.

"I want to see my daughter."

"It's not a good time right now, Brenda."

"Why are you keeping me from seeing her?" Why are you doing this to me?"

"Brenda, I love you. You're my own mother, you know that."

Click.

Jack is more forgiving. At least outwardly. More used to hiding pain.

"She's going to be OK?"

"We're doing everything we can to make that happen. We've got the best doctors. She's getting the best treatment."

"Her mother's worried, you know. She wants to come down there and see for herself."

"It's just not the right time. I'll call you. I know how hard this is."

Click.

Cailin's angry with me. I see it in her eyes. I see the way she dashes by me in the morning on the way to school. Just a cursory wave. If I'm there, and she has to kiss me good-bye, it's brief. Barely making contact. A bitter butterfly kiss.

One day, about three years later, when Diana was OK again, Cailin and I were alone in the kitchen having breakfast. Out of nowhere, she just started crying hysterically.

"She could have died! You never told me! You never let me know that."

"I was just trying to protect . . ."

Screaming now, "You never told me the truth, Dad. You shut me out. She could have died. Right . . . ? Right."

Then me, softly, in response. "That's right."

"How close did she come? Tell me now. How close?"

"Close."

I tell Cailin I'm sorry. I did the best I could. I did what I thought was best for Diana. Diana didn't want anyone in the family to know the odds. To talk about the "what ifs." She never wanted to weigh the options or discuss the alternatives. It was almost as if acknowledging the possibility of "failure" would allow "failure" to step into the room with us. Become part of our equation. And for Diana, it never was an option.

Shana has a different perspective, which she shares with me a few years later.

"Don't take this the wrong way, Dad, OK? And you know we love you both the same. But, I guess we all thought you would be the one to go first. And it would be better that way."

"Oh?"

"Well, again, don't take this the wrong way. And you know we love you both the same. But, we always thought that Mom, although she'd be heartbroken, could probably continue to live her life."

"Uh-huh."

"And don't take this the wrong way. And you know we love you both the same. But if Mom did, God forbid, go first, we didn't think you could go on."

Smart girl. At least she's been paying attention.

Slowly now, agonizingly slowly, Diana's numbers start to improve. Or at least stabilize. Her CPK number, which measures inflammation in the body, has been off the charts. Normal's about 150 and she's been hovering around 11,000. But we've been able to cut that in half now.

She's still taking very large doses of prednisone, and she's beginning to exhibit some definitely odd characteristics. She doesn't sleep much at night. And she's started channeling the universe through a very funny voice she's been communicating with. Whoever this guy is, I think he definitely played the Catskills at one time, because Diana's suddenly a fountain of one-liners. She's also getting very specific commentary from this guy about me, and her, and our kids, and our mission here on earth, and our connection to the universe.

One night around three A.M. I get up and try to quietly slip out of bed.

"Where are you going?" she asks, wide awake.

"I'm going to the bathroom."

"By yourself?"

"Yeah, some people are still able to do that."

"Hurry back. I have to talk to you."

"What?"

"I checked your messages with the universe. I've got something for you."

When I come back, I sit across from her on my chair.

"What's up?" I ask her, wide awake myself now. "What's the big message?"

"Call Michael Fox, and make up with him. I won't get better if you don't do that. And neither will he."

I don't respond at first.

"If you don't, it's going to make *you* sick too. I can see how unhappy you are about it. There's an emptiness you have to fill. Call him tomorrow. You love him."

In the morning, I pick up the phone and call Michael in New York. We haven't spoken in at least ten months.

"Mike."

"Hi, Gary."

I can hear the nervousness in his voice. Can feel the tension. I'm very nervous myself.

"Mike, this can't be the way our story ends. With us not friends. It just can't."

"I don't want it to be that way either." Softly from Mike. Sweetly.

"Here's the thing, I don't care who's right or wrong. I love you. I'll always love you, and I want you back in my life."

There's silence. And then I realize that Michael's crying, and he can't talk.

Then, we're overlapping.

"My fault."

"My fault."

"I'm sorry."

"I'm sorry."

"My fault."

Toppling all over each other with apologies. Happy to hear each other's voice again.

Mike's crying. I'm crying. This "thing" has been killing us. Eating us up. Causing Mike pain when he can least afford it. When he needs all our love and prayers. And now I can add my prayers to those of the rest of the world. This "thing" is over.

"I'll call you."

"Give my love to the family."

"Surrender to win." A long way from "eat the meat to beat the house."

Meanwhile, on another stage, the "life and death" battle for the existence of the Archer School plays out. We have prevailed, so far, at every level in the legal process. But after each verdict, the "Concerned Citizens" have appealed. No matter how scathing the criticism of them and their behavior, no matter how tenuous their legal standing in each ruling, they continue to spend ungodly sums of money in the appeal process, forcing us to match them. Perhaps they hope we'll run out of money, or patience. We won't.

It is now the day of the city council vote, which will be the final decision in this grueling process. And not subject to appeal. Even though our psychic friend has predicted success, we're obviously nervous.

The city council chambers are impressive, ornate and gilded. The room is filled with Archer supporters on one side of the chamber. Opponents of Archer on the other. Each glaring across the aisle. Like a Hatfield-and-McCoy wedding.

I have wheeled Diana up to the front door of the council chamber But, she wants to get out and leave the wheelchair here.

"I don't want to see it in my memory of this moment."

When her friends see her "walk" in, they begin to cry. Happy tears. As far as I can tell, crying is a routine event at girls' schools. And among girls'-school supporters. There's also a lot of hugging and petting, and a lot of tea. All of which we see inside the council hall.

Speeches are made. Lies retold. Questions asked and answered. When the time comes, we hold our breath and hold each other's hands. The city council vote is 13–0 in our favor. With several of the council members going out of their way to heap praise on the Archer School, and its mission to educate young girls from all walks of life, from all the neighborhoods of Los Angeles.

The cheers from our side mingle with the tears. I hug Diana. I cry a little myself. I have some tea. The Archer School will live.

There's still, however, the little matter of the fourteen million dollars to buy the Eastern Star Home. *Spin City* has been sold into syndication, but it will be a few years before I actually see any of my profit share. And at this point it isn't quite clear what the total revenue will be. Or precisely when it will arrive.

I go to Katzenberg to ask for help. I need an advance. He points out the uncertainties, the unknowns. It's all set, yes. But it's not "set-set,"* as they say.

"Then I need a favor."

Jeffrey has to speak with his partners. He'll get back.

The clock is ticking. If we don't deliver the money, we'll be in breach. Not only will we lose the building, we'll be sued. Two days before the deadline, Jeffrey Katzenberg gives me a check for fourteen million dollars. I give it to Diana to give to Archer, and she, of course, cries. I cry again too—what the hell. And ask her for a cup of tea.

In December, Diana goes in to see Dr. Metzger for a final series of tests. It's been the year from hell, almost exactly, but she's been progressing for several months now. We have a surprise for Dr. Metzger, as Diana walks in all by herself for these tests. The first time he's ever seen her out of the wheelchair. Dr. Metzger cries and does a silly little "Jewish-guy" dance, part twist and part hora. And he smiles through his tears.

When the test results are ready, Betsy has taken the message from Dr. Metzger's office. She leaves me a note.

> G,
> *Diana's tests came back.*
> *They're all perfect.*
> B

I frame the note and put it on my desk. Where it still sits.

---

*William Goldman's concept from the brilliant book *Adventures in the Screen Trade*.

1969

{ c h a p t e r   t w e n t y - s i x }

Now Orleans is like a 3-D movie, and we're overwhelmed by sight and sound and color. Music everywhere. Sweet smells and raucous laughter. It was difficult maneuvering the big, yellow Hertz truck down the narrow streets. But we've made it safely to our destination. Since it's Christmas Eve, we've decided to splurge and sleep indoors tonight, and we've found a small, cheap but cheerful motel on the outskirts of the French Quarter.

Darkness is falling now, and I feel sad for Diana. This is so different from the Christmas Eves she knew at home. She's going to go out to walk around a little. I'm tired from driving, so I'm going to stay and take a little nap. Diana wants to go to midnight Mass later, and I told her, since it will be my first time, I want to be well rested, to be able to take it all in. Maybe I'll convert. Who knows? A Christmas miracle.

When I wake up, there's a kind of resin-y smell to the little motel room. There are colored lights blinking on and off. And I hear what sounds like . . . a little steam engine.

My eyes focus, and I see the magic that Diana's conjured up. In our room is a tiny Christmas tree, with ornaments and colored lights. Going around the little tree is a very little electric train. There's a Merry Christmas sign up on our window. And as she sees me come awake she rings a bell.

"Merry Christmas." She laughs.

Seems she went around town and begged, borrowed, and cajoled her way into old toys that maybe were going to be thrown out anyway. A string of lights, with some broken. This tiny tree, which no one was going to take. And then the train set, which is scratched and has a wheel missing. She got it all for our last twenty dollars, but a better investment we will never make. We're broke. But we're having Christmas.

She wants to apologize for the threadbare items. The "blinky" lights. The scrawny tree. It's the window at Macy's as far as I'm concerned.

We lie in bed watching our train go around our tree.

"My own electric train set. Finally."

"It's not too late to go to medical school, you know."

"When we get back to California, I'd like to get a dog," I say, still flush in the Christmas spirit, and feeling about eight years old.

"Great. What kind of dog, do you think?"

"I like those big, black dogs. They're called Labradors, I think."

"I love Labs."

There's a moment of blissful silence.

"What do you want to call him?" she asks.

"I don't know. Rex? Spot?"

She looks over at me and smiles indulgently as she pats the top of my head.

"We'll think of something."

"Rover?"

"Shh."

And I have to face the fact now, it's official. I'm in love.

2006

{ c h a p t e r t w e n t y - s e v e n }

On Yom Kippur this year, I receive a large check in the mail—my quarterly profit share on *Spin City,* which is in wide syndication all around the world. I didn't know you were allowed to receive mail on Yom Kippur, let alone mail with large profit checks inside. The old Bensonhurst neighborhood completely closed down for the Jewish high holidays, where it was a very big deal. In Vermont, where Diana and I live now, Yom Kippur's a big deal for me and the Berkowitz twins up in Rutland, which is pretty much the Vermont Jewish community.*

I call Mike Fox to check in, and we celebrate our good fortune. After our estrangement in New York, ten years ago now, we don't take our relationship for granted. It's precious. And we almost lost it. And every few months, one of us seems to call to say, "How are you? How're you feelin'? What're you thinking about?" It's like being married, without sex.

I was in New York City recently, and Mike and I had lunch. He, sweetly, took me out to a French brasserie on the Upper East Side. An homage to the old days at Saint Germain. But this time it was Diet Cokes and iced teas. And the talk was about kids and schools.

And the talk was also, of course, about politics. And about

---

*The number of Jewish people in Vermont is approximately 5,500, the same as in my gym class at Lafayette.

stem-cell research. And the glorious impact of Mike's political advocacy this year, in support of candidates who were pro stem-cell research.

Just about everywhere Mike went to campaign, those candidates were victorious. With the work of the MJF Foundation, which has raised more than 100 million dollars blazing new trails, Mike has transformed the landscape of scientific research in this country. And he is as firmly convinced as ever that this disease will be eradicated in his lifetime. And that he will indeed dance at his daughter's wedding.

I am in awe of Mike. Of his courage. His determination. Of his dignity. And I have no reason to doubt him. I'm lucky to be his friend.

It's the tenth anniversary, as well, of the Archer School this year. Up and down Sunset Boulevard, where there used to be the NO TO ARCHER signs, there are now beautiful banners lining both sides of the broad boulevard proclaiming, ARCHER SCHOOL FOR GIRLS — CELEBRATING TEN YEARS OF EXCELLENCE.

Dr. Sally Ride is the graduation speaker. She's funny. She's charming. Brilliant. We know she's brave. She would be a perfect Archer student. There are 501 girls in the school now, up from the 33 we started with. In the front row, I see three of our scholarship kids, two African-American girls and one Latina. Cornell, Brown, Princeton. We got Amherst for the first time this year. Swarthmore. Diana hands out the diplomas. She cries. She looks at me. I cry. Why not?

From my front porch in Vermont, I have a clear view across the valley over to the Green Mountains about forty miles away. We live in an old farmhouse, which sits on top of a hill at the end of a long and winding country road. On the sign at the bottom of the hill there's a picture of Ubu. Instead of his Frisbee he carries a maple leaf.

Diana and I get to spend all day together. No computer. No

e-mail. No cell phones. We seem to be the only two people in America who can't figure out how to work our TiVo. And we reside very comfortably once again outside the mainstream of American culture. It's very much our old '60s life, but with a nice roof over our heads this time around.

Dr. Metzger comes to visit us this summer. It's so great to have him here with us. We eat homemade pie. Drink homemade apple cider. Have vegetables and salad from the garden. Take long walks through the woods.

"Why'd she get better?" I ask him. "What happened? Why'd it work?"

Metzger shrugs. He's not really sure.

"Good patient," he tells me.

"Good doctor," I say to him.

He laughs, smiles modestly.

"And luck. . . . A lot of goddamn luck."

We leave it at that.

The Brooklyn guys come up to play basketball at least once a year. Our old coach, Gil Fershtman, the best coach I ever played for, the Grant Tinker of coaches, comes too. And he's still coaching us.

One time, I drive to the basket and end up taking and missing a very awkward shot. Gil calls me to the side.

"Gary, when you're going to the basket that way, and you're covered, you need to look and see if you can't dish off," he counsels.

"Coach, I'm sixty-two years old. All I have left is 'go' or 'don't go.' I don't have 'go and dish.'"

He agrees to cut me some slack. But I can see he's not happy with my shot selection.

We play all weekend. The game has slowed to a crawl, but it's still fun. There are a lot more knee braces and back braces involved. There's a portable defibrillator lying on the grass. But it's still fun.

Afterward, we drink and tell stories, always the same stories, into the wee hours. Someone inevitably will bring up the Wingate game, now a scant forty-four years ago.

"You didn't foul that guy, Fred."

"No way."

"Bad call."

"Fuck that ref."

Diana has elevated our sports stories from complete bullshit, which is what a lot of the other wives think they are, to "ritual communication," which sounds so much more important. And like something you could even study in school.

"It's your oral history," she explains to the boys. "It's the way you pass down the legends of your tribe. And it's important that the stories be told and retold exactly the same way each year."

All the other wives groan and throw their napkins at her.

But Coach is nodding his head and crying softly, he's so happy.

I look over at these guys, whom I have known for fifty years, some of whom were at my bar mitzvah, and my heart skips a beat. And I remember. In the days when I was "floundering," as my dad would say. I remember twenty dollars coming in the mail, anonymously. Ten-dollar bills stuffed into my backpack after a visit, anonymously. Clothes coming in the mail, for baby Shana at Christmastime, anonymously. Not so anonymously that I couldn't figure it out. From these guys. From my brother. How lucky am I to know them.

When company's gone, Diana and I walk through the woods with our five dogs. Four Newfoundlands and a Labrador. We're on dog time. We nap a lot. We lie in the sun. We roll over. Whatever that was, my time in the show-business world, it feels like it's over. Whatever drove me to want to express myself that way. To give myself up to that obsession of doing a weekly TV show. That passion's gone. I loved TV. I have great memories. Great friends. I don't think anybody ever had as much fun. But, I don't want to put that much energy and focus into anything anymore, other than Diana, and the kids, and the dogs.

I watch my two beautiful daughters deal with the world they are born into. Shana, extremely talented and successful, still holds on proudly to the memory of her Berkeley hippie roots. One day, gently mocking her younger sister's gilded early childhood, she tells her, "You know, I didn't have a nanny. My nanny's name was freedom."

Shana grows into a sweet, compassionate, and thoughtful woman. In 1992, her sophomore year at college back East, I had to go to NYC to attend a funeral. Diana had a prior commitment to speak at a conference up in Oregon, so I was going to be all by myself down in the city. Shana called me from school. She was worried about me being without Mom at such a stressful time. Did I want her to come down to New York and be with me? I said, "Yes." I really did. And she came.

That night we went out to dinner at the Cornelia Street Café down in the Village. Not far from where Diana and I spent the early days and nights of our relationship. Shana was so solicitous of me and how I was feeling. So supportive. So intelligent and engaged. I remember thinking if I didn't know this young woman and I had just met her, I would be so thrilled to have made her acquaintance.

Born in 1983, Cailin's life experience has been one of ease and entitlement from the day she was born. Nannies, private school, Ivy League. This was to be Cailin's life. One time I told her I felt bad that we had robbed her of the thrill of being young and poor. She said not to worry. Young and rich was working very well for her, thank you.

It's been interesting watching her navigate her way through this life. Early on, she figured out how to get what she wanted from each of her parents. For her mother, the magic words were "strong female role model." That worked for bikes and later cars, trains, and anything that you could build stuff with.

For me, she knew the magic words "It's for the family."

"All these Barbie dolls and My Little Ponys are for the family?"

"Yes. For my cousins when they come to visit."

"All your cousins are boys."

"Don't stereotype by gender, Dad."

What eight-year-old knows *stereotype?* Or, *gender?*

Cailin was always sweet and generous and loving. And funny. Once during a difficult period we were going through, I realized something about the two of us.

"You know what it is?" I told her. "I really resent the fact that you have wealthy parents."

Cailin nodded. "Hopefully, you can understand how that's not my fault."

Money changes everything. People who don't believe that haven't seen enough money. Most of it, beyond a doubt, is a very, very good change. But some of it is murky. I had to find a way to deal with this "life jump." A place to put it that wouldn't make it seem like a betrayal of my father. A betrayal of my neighborhood. My friends. Like I was trying to be "somebody." Like I was reading the *New York Times.*

For me now, money buys me time, a precious gift. And it keeps stupid people out of my life. I don't spend two minutes a day, ever, with someone I don't want to be with. I'm never in a position where I have to falsely flatter anyone. Or, where I'll allow anyone to falsely flatter me.

It's been my great good fortune to always be in my proper time. In the '50s, growing up in Brooklyn, I was a sports-crazed, uncomplicated, narrow-minded kid in a world that seemed to value sports-crazed, uncomplicated narrowness.

In the '60s, as the fabric of society was breaking open, I was right there at the heart of it in Greenwich Village. And then later on in Berkeley. And I didn't leave much on the table untested or untried. It would be easier to start with a list of things I didn't do.

I also began, at that time, to expand my own ideas about friendship and tolerance. About what it is to be a man. To be a woman. To be a family.

The '70s were about starting our own family. And we did.

The '80s were about making money. And we made a lot.

The '90s were about giving it back. And we've tried our hardest.

And now we're waiting for the '00s to reveal their purpose to us.

But if you wake me in the middle of the night and shake me and ask me who I am, I will tell you. I'm a kid from Brooklyn whose father worked in the post office. And one day at a party, the gods smiled on me as I walked over to a beautiful young woman who had just finished singing a folk song. I gathered up my courage, and I gave her my best line:

"Nice guitar," I said.

{ a c k n o w l e d g m e n t s }

*O*n a cross-country plane trip back east, Geoff Cowan and Aileen Adams spent the Denver-to-Chicago portion of the flight trying to convince me to put my stories and my story into book form. And somewhere over Lake Erie, I managed to put my fears aside and agreed to at least give it a try. Hopefully, this is close to what they had in mind.

Lisa Bankoff, of the nonprofit ICM Agency in New York, read the first fifty pages I scribbled, offered to represent the book, and has done so with style and grace, quickly making the transition from agent to friend. And valued deeply in both roles.

The folks at Harmony, Shaye Areheart and my editor Julia Pastore, have showered this book with affection and respect and good grammar. And they helped make this a much stronger book, I believe, than the one I laid upon their doorstep.

A special thank-you to my earliest readers—Sam Weisman, Suzanne Todd, Claire Cook. At my most vulnerable moments, you propped me up, cheered me on, gave me reason to believe. Agreed to read another draft. And then another. And then one more.

At critical moments, with my confidence waning, Roy Furman and Jenny Gersten each stepped in and offered encouragement and insight, and promised there would be at least two people who would buy this book.

Deep and heartfelt thanks to friends who inspired me throughout this process: Bernie Bandman, Ceil Bandman, Alan Bergman, Marilyn Bergman, Skip Brittenham, Ben Cardinale, Diane Cooke, John Cooke, Dorothy Fielding, Brad Hall, Alan Horn, Cindy Horn, Jeffrey Katzenberg, Kathy Kennedy, Dan Klores, Jon LaPook, Marc Lawrence, Julia Louis-Dreyfus, Frank Marshall, Marcia Mazria, Allan Metzger, Pat Mitchell, Kathryn Peters, Tracy Pollan, Peter Schneider, Susan Seeger, Scott Seydel, Steven Spielberg, Grant Tinker, Jennifer Todd, Marc Tucker, Michael Weithorn. I could never have completed this without your support and guidance.

Diana, my father was right.

Thank you, Michael Fox. Which is what I say each night before I go to bed.

"ShanaCailin," I promise I can actually tell the two of you apart. But, I love you both the same.

My brother, Stan, still my hero. Thanks for "pitching 'em in." My "sister," Starr. Thanks for coming to my bar mitzvah and leading the bunny hop. And for always being on my side.

Coach Gil, sorry I took so many shots and didn't play better defense. But, we can't fix that now, and I think we have to move on.

Fred, you did not foul that guy.

Thanks to Heather Green, my assistant, the only person in the world who can read my handwriting. Your generous spirit always lifted my own.

Thank you, Maria, who sees all, for helping me put the events of my life into a larger context. And forcing me to try and live up to my responsibilities, as I had promised.

Anyone working in network television today owes a debt of gratitude to Norman Lear for redefining and expanding the idea of what a television show could be about. And be. Thank you, Norman.

Finally, I've always felt that people who write memoirs make themselves out to be better than they actually were in real life. I'm confident I have not violated that tradition.

Gary David Goldberg was born in Brooklyn, New York, on June 25, 1944. After a prolonged and checkered collegiate career, which began at Brandeis University in 1962 and ended at San Diego State University in 1975 (with several other schools in between), he moved to Hollywood to try to make it as a writer.

Mr. Goldberg has been the recipient of numerous honors during his career, including two Emmy Awards, two Golden Globes, six Humanitas Prizes, a Peabody, a Christopher, two Viewers for Quality Television Awards, the Producers Guild Award as Producer of the Year in 1991 and the Writers Guild of America's Valentine Davies Award in 1998 for his contributions to the entertainment industry. In 2002 he won the Award of Excellence at Banff's World Television Festival, and in 2003 he was honored with the Outstanding Television Writer Award at the Austin Film Festival. Mr. Goldberg is a member of the Broadcasting Magazine Hall of Fame.

He lives in Vermont with his wife Dr. Diana Meehan and their five dogs.

Visit him at www.GaryDavidGoldberg.com